SCOTT FORESMAN · ADDISON WESLEY

Mathematics

Grade 2

Every Student Learns

With a Foreword by Dr. Jim Cummins

ESL Consultant
Darrel Nickolaisen
Teacher/Consultant
Apple Valley, California

Editorial Offices: Glenview, Illinois • Parsippany, New Jersey • New York, New York

Sales Offices: Parsippany, New Jersey • Duluth, Georgia • Glenview, Illinois
Coppell, Texas • Ontario, California • Mesa, Arizona

i

Overview

Every Student Learns is a lesson-by-lesson companion to
Scott Foresman - Addison Wesley Mathematics and Matemáticas Scott
Foresman - Addison Wesley. It has been designed to provide manageable
support for teachers and their students who are challenged by language issues in
Mathematics, no matter what the first language may be.

Every Student Learns is built upon the Three Pillars of English Language Learning
in the Content Areas by Dr. Jim Cummins of the University of Toronto:

• Activate Prior Knowledge/Build Background

• Access Content

• Extend Language

ISBN: 0-328-07551-5

8 9 10   V004 09 08 07 06

Table of Contents

Supporting ESL Students
in Learning the Language of Mathematics

DR. JIM CUMMINS • UNIVERSITY OF TORONTO

Mathematics and Language

Mathematics can legitimately be considered to be a language in itself in that it employs symbols to represent concepts, symbols that facilitate our thinking about aspects of reality. However, mathematics is also intimately related to the natural language that we begin to acquire as infants, the language we use to communicate in a variety of everyday and academic contexts. Mathematics and language are interconnected at several levels:

• Teachers use natural language to explain mathematical concepts and perform mathematical operations. Students who have limited proficiency in English require additional support in order to understand mathematical concepts and operations taught in English. Among the supports that teachers can use to make instruction comprehensible for English language learners are demonstrations; concrete, hands-on manipulatives and graphic organizers; simplification and paraphrasing of instructional language; and direct teaching of key vocabulary.

• As is the case in other academic disciplines, mathematics uses a specialized technical vocabulary to represent concepts and, in the case of mathematics, describe operations. As early as Grade 1, students are required to learn the meanings of such words as *addition, subtraction, sum,* and *addend,* words that are likely to be found only in mathematics discourse. Furthermore, other terms have specific meanings in mathematics discourse that differ from their meanings in everyday usage and in other subject areas. Examples of these kinds of terms include words such as *table, product, even,* and *odd.* Homophones such as *sum* and *some* may also be confusing for ESL students. Grade 1 students are required to learn key concepts, such as *number facts* and *addition sentences,* at a time when many of them (ESL students, in particular) may not know the broader meanings of words such as *facts* and *sentences.*

• In addition to the technical vocabulary of mathematics, language intersects with mathematics at the broader level of general vocabulary, syntax, semantics, and discourse. Most mathematical problems require students to understand propositions and logical relations that are expressed through language. Consider this problem at the Grade 4 level:

> *Wendy gave a total of 10 treats to her dogs. She gave her large dog 2 more treats than she gave her small dog. How many treats did she give to each dog?*

Here students need to understand (or be able to figure out) the meanings of words such as *total* and *treats.* They need to understand the logical relation expressed by the *more … than …* construction. And they need to infer that Wendy has only two dogs, even though this fact is not explicitly included in the problem. Clearly, the language demands of the math curriculum increase as students progress through the grades, and these demands can cause particular difficulties for ESL students.

The ESL Challenge

Numerous research studies have demonstrated that ESL students generally require at least 5 years to catch up to native speakers in academic language proficiency (i.e., reading and writing skills; see Cummins, 2001 for a review). In mathematics, ESL students often make good progress in acquiring basic computation skills in the early grades. However, they typically experience greater difficulty in learning to interpret and solve word problems, and this difficulty increases in the later elementary grades as the word problems become more linguistically and conceptually complex.

These developmental patterns can be understood in relation to three very different aspects of language proficiency:

- **Conversational fluency** is the ability to carry on a conversation in familiar face-to-face situations. This is the kind of proficiency that the vast majority of native speakers of English have developed by the time they enter school at age 5. It involves the use of high-frequency words and simple grammatical constructions. ESL students generally develop basic fluency in conversational aspects of English within a year or two of exposure to the language, either within school or in their out-of-school environments.

- **Discrete language skills** reflect specific phonological, lexical, and grammatical knowledge that students can acquire in two ways: (a) as a result of direct instruction and (b) through both formal and informal practice (e.g., reading). Some of these discrete language skills are acquired early in schooling, and some continue to be acquired throughout schooling. The discrete language skills that are acquired early include knowledge of the letters of the alphabet, the sounds represented by individual letters and combinations of letters, and the ability to decode written words and pronounce them appropriately. ESL students can learn these specific language skills at a relatively early stage in their acquisition of English; in fact, these skills can be learned concurrently with their development of basic vocabulary and conversational proficiency.

  In mathematics, these discrete language skills include knowledge of the symbols that represent basic mathematical operations (e.g., + and –), the terms used to refer to these symbols and operations (*add, subtract, plus, minus,* etc.), and the basic technical vocabulary of mathematics. Clearly, the ability to decode written text is also a necessary (but not a sufficient) condition for thinking through and solving word problems expressed in written language.

- **Academic language proficiency** includes knowledge of the less frequent vocabulary of English as well as the ability to interpret and produce increasingly complex written language. As students progress through the grades, they encounter far more low-frequency words (primarily from Greek and Latin sources), complex syntax (e.g., the passive voice), and abstract expressions that are virtually never heard in everyday conversation. Students are required to understand linguistically and conceptually demanding texts in the content areas (e.g., literature, social studies, science, and mathematics) and to use this increasingly sophisticated language in accurate and coherent ways in their own writing.

Acquiring academic language proficiency is challenging for all students. Schools spend at least 12 years trying to extend the conversational language that native-speaking children bring to school into these more complex academic language spheres. It is hardly surprising, therefore, that research has repeatedly shown that ESL students usually require at least 5 years of exposure to academic English in order to catch up to native-speaker norms. In addition to internalizing increasingly complex academic language, ESL students must catch up to a moving target. Every year, native speakers are making large gains in their reading and writing abilities and in their knowledge of vocabulary. In order to catch up to grade norms within 6 years, ESL students must make 15 months' gain in every 10-month school year. By contrast, the typical native-speaking student is expected to make 10 months' gain in a 10-month school year (Collier & Thomas, 1999).

All three aspects of language proficiency are important. However, the three aspects—conversational fluency, discrete language skills, and academic language proficiency—are frequently confused by policy makers and by the media. For example, it is sometimes claimed that children acquire language rapidly and that one year of instructional support is sufficient to enable ESL students to catch up academically. In reality, many ESL students who have acquired fluent conversational skills are still a long way from grade-level performance in academic language proficiency (e.g., in reading comprehension in content areas such as math).

Similarly, the learning of discrete language skills does not generalize automatically to academic language proficiency. ESL (and native-speaking) students who can "read" a mathematical problem fluently may have only a very limited understanding of the words and sentences they can decode.

Thus, ESL students may require extended language support within the classroom in order to continue to make grade-level progress in content areas such as mathematics. Despite the fact that these students have acquired conversational fluency in English, together with basic mathematical vocabulary and computational skills, they may still experience gaps in their knowledge of some of the more sophisticated vocabulary, syntax, and discursive features of mathematical language.

Teaching the Language of Mathematics

From an instructional perspective, the relationship between language and mathematics is both two-way and reciprocal. Mathematical knowledge is developed through language, and language abilities can and should be developed through mathematics instruction. Specifically:

- Because mathematical concepts and operations are embedded in language, the specialized vocabulary of mathematics and the discursive features of mathematical propositions must be taught explicitly if students are to make strong academic progress in mathematics.

- Equally important, however, is the fact that in teaching mathematics, we are also developing and reinforcing students' general academic language proficiency. For example, think about the language learning that will likely occur as the teacher explains the following Grade 1 problem to a group of ESL students.

   Is 3 + 8 greater than 10, equal to 10, or less than 10? Explain.

Students will learn not only the specific meanings of the terms *greater than, equal to,* and l*ess than,* but also synonyms for these terms (e.g., a synonym for *great* is *big,* and the meaning of *greater than* is similar to the meaning of *bigger than*). This particular mathematics problem also presents the teacher an opportunity to teach students the general concept of *comparatives* and the general rule for forming comparatives (e.g., *great, greater, greatest; big, bigger, biggest*). The fact that not all comparatives take exactly these forms can also be taught in relation to *less, lesser, least.* Finally, the meaning of the word explain can be taught (e.g., *describe, tell about, tell why you think so*) and related to its use in other subject areas (e.g., science).

The reciprocal interdependence of language and mathematics becomes apparent, and even obvious, when perusing any mathematics textbook. Much of what students are expected to learn in mathematics is presented in written text. Students are required to read the text in order to develop their understanding of math concepts and their ability to solve math problems. Frequently, students are also required to explain orally or in writing how they solved a particular problem. Obviously, teachers and students will discuss these concepts; but without strong reading skills, students will find it very difficult to acquire, and truly assimilate, lesson content. Without strong writing skills, they will have difficulty demonstrating their knowledge of the concepts and skills that they are often, in fact, acquiring. Thus, effective reading and writing skills are necessary for students to make progress in mathematics, particularly as they move through the elementary grades. By the same token, the teaching of mathematics provides important opportunities for teachers to model academic language in their interactions with students and also to teach features of academic language directly (e.g., reading comprehension strategies, comparative adjectives, and context- or content-specific vocabulary).

Effective academic language instruction for ESL students across the curriculum is built on three fundamental pillars:

- **Activate Prior Knowledge/Build Background**
- **Access Content**
- **Extend Language**

In developing mathematical knowledge through language, and language abilities through mathematics, we can apply these three instructional principles in powerful ways.

Activate Prior Knowledge/Build Background

A. Prior knowledge as the foundation of learning
There is general agreement among cognitive psychologists that we learn by integrating new input into our existing cognitive structures or schemata. Our prior experience provides the foundation for interpreting new information. No learner is a blank slate. In fact, learning can be defined as the process of relating new information to the information we already possess. When we read a mathematical problem, for example, we construct meaning by bringing our prior knowledge of language, of mathematics, and of the world in general to the text. Our prior knowledge enables us to make inferences about the meanings of words and expressions that we may not have encountered before. As our prior knowledge expands through new learning, we are enabled to understand a greater range of mathematical concepts and also the language that expresses those concepts.

Thus, a major rationale for activating students' prior knowledge (or if there is minimal prior knowledge on a particular topic or issue, building it with students), is to make the learning process more efficient. It is important to *activate* students' prior knowledge because students may not explicitly realize what they know about a particular topic or issue; consequently, their prior knowledge may not facilitate learning unless it is brought to an immediate, and conscious, level.

B. Prior knowledge and ESL students

In a classroom that includes second-language learners from diverse backgrounds, prior knowledge about a particular topic may vary widely. Thus, simple transmission of certain information or a given skill will fail to connect with the prior knowledge and previous experience of many students. As a result, the input will be much less comprehensible for these students. Some students may have relevant information in their first language (L1), but not realize that there is any connection with what they are learning in English (L2). In other cases, the algorithms and strategies that students have acquired for carrying out math operations in their countries of origin may differ considerably from the procedures they are now being taught in English. Clearly, these discrepancies can cause confusion for students.

In teaching math to ESL students, it is important that we attempt to connect the instruction both with students' prior experience of learning math and with their prior knowledge of the world in general. In building up our own knowledge of students' educational and cultural backgrounds, we can collaborate with ESL teachers, who may have greater access to this information, and also with community volunteers, who can often provide invaluable insights about students' prior learning and cultural knowledge.

Lois Meyer (2000) has expressed clearly the importance of prior knowledge (familiarity with a given topic) in reducing the cognitive load of instruction for ESL students. She notes that the notion of *cognitive load* refers to the number and complexity of new concepts embedded in a particular lesson or text. This cognitive load depends not only on the text itself but also on the students' prior knowledge of the content.

> If the English learner has little entry knowledge about the subject matter, the cognitive load of the lesson will be heavy, for many concepts will be new and unfamiliar. The student will have little basis from which to generate hypotheses regarding the meanings the teacher is conveying through English.

> If the student's entry knowledge of the topic is considerable, this will lighten the cognitive load. Learners can draw on their knowledge to interpret linguistic and non-linguistic clues in the lesson in order to make educated guesses about the meanings of the teacher's talk and text (2000, p. 229).

Clearly, the cognitive load of many mathematical texts is considerable, particularly as students progress through the grades. Finding out what students know about a particular topic allows the teacher to supply relevant concepts or vocabulary that some or all students may be lacking, but which will be important for understanding the upcoming text or lesson. Building this context permits students to understand more complex language and to pursue more cognitively demanding activities. It lessens the cognitive load of the text and frees up students' brain power.

C. Strategies for Activating Prior Knowledge and Building Background

Three types of prior knowledge are relevant to consider in teaching mathematics: prior knowledge of math; knowledge that has been acquired through direct experiences; and knowledge acquired through secondary sources (e.g. books, videos, etc.). We can use brainstorming, role playing, and simulations, as well as connections to literature and other content areas to activate students' prior knowledge and build relevant background knowledge.

- **Connect to Prior Knowledge of Math** In Grade 1 we might activate students' knowledge of counting as a prelude to teaching them to use *counting on* as a tool for addition. Or at the Grade 4 level, we might activate students' knowledge of basic multiplication facts in order to reinforce the foundation for teaching more complex multiplication operations.

- **Connect to Prior Knowledge of Language** Although mathematics has its own technical language that students must learn, we explain this language, and the associated math operations, using more familiar everyday language. For example, in explaining the concept of *subtraction* we will use high frequency expressions such as *take away from* that are likely to be much more familiar to children. Typically, the meaning of this language will be reinforced through demonstrations involving concrete manipulatives or graphic organizers.

- **Connect to Prior Experiences** We can find out from students what activities they engage in outside of school and link mathematics instruction to those activities (e.g., students who engage in various sports can carry out a variety of operations relevant to those sports, such as calculating, comparing, and contrasting batting averages). We can also be proactive in *creating experiences* for students that will promote mathematical knowledge and skill. For example, we might engage parents as collaborators by having them work with their children in calculating the proportion of weekly food expenditures that the family spends on the various food groups, thereby reinforcing both social studies and math concepts.

- **Use Brainstorming, Role Playing, and Simulation** At a very early age most children develop an intuitive sense of "fairness" and an ability to judge whether goods of various kinds (e.g., toys or treats) have been distributed equally or fairly. We can use brainstorming, role-playing, and simulation to carry out a variety of math activities that tap into students' real-life experiences of equal (or fair) distribution. In the early grades, we would likely use concrete manipulatives to support these activities. In intermediate grades, real or simulated data can be used.

We can also link math to the development of critical thinking by having students carry out projects that go beyond the curriculum in various ways. For example, in a class with many ESL students we might have students brainstorm about the languages they know and how they learned them. On the basis of this brainstorming, they could then develop a questionnaire and carry out a more formal survey of the linguistic make-up of the class (or even the entire school). In analyzing data that reflect their own experiences and identities, students' motivation to explore effective analytic strategies and presentation tools (e.g., graphs and computerized slide shows) is likely to be considerably greater than when the activities are more distant from their experiences and interests.

- **Use Literature and Connections to Content** Relatively few people in North America have ever been in a jungle, but most adults and children can describe the main features of jungles as a result of secondary experiences of various sorts. In the classroom, we can use literature, high-interest expository texts, and other forms of media (e.g., videotapes) both to activate students' prior knowledge of math and also to build background knowledge.

In some cases, connecting to prior experiences will involve use of stories that have been specifically selected because they contain relevant math content. In other cases, we will connect math concepts and operations to other subject matter across the curriculum. For example, we might link math to a social studies unit on government as we discuss where local and state governments get the funds to operate and as we have students calculate the sales taxes that their families pay for various kinds of purchases.

The essential point here is that the more connections we can make both to students' experiences and interests and to other areas of the curriculum, the more relevance math is likely to assume in students' minds and lives. This, in turn, will result in more powerful learning of math.

An additional consideration in activating ESL Students' prior knowledge is that this process communicates a sense of respect for what students already know and an interest in their cultural backgrounds. This affirmation of students' identities increases students' personal and academic confidence and motivates them to invest their identities more strongly in pursuing academic success.

Access Content

How can teachers make the complex language of mathematics comprehensible for students who are still in the process of learning English? How can students be enabled to take ownership of their learning of math concepts and operations rather than just learn rote procedures? One important strategy has already been noted in the previous section. Activating and building students' background knowledge is an essential part of the process of helping students to participate academically and gain access to meaning. When we activate students' prior knowledge we attempt to modify the "soil" so that the seeds of meaning can take root. However, we can also support or *scaffold* students' learning by modifying the input itself. We provide this scaffolding by embedding the content in a *richly redundant context* wherein there are multiple routes to the mathematical meaning at hand in addition to the language itself.

The following list presents a variety of ways of modifying the presentation of mathematical content to ESL students so that they can more effectively get access to the meaning in any given lesson.

- **Use Demonstration** Teachers can take students through a word problem in math, demonstrating step-by-step procedures and strategies in a clear and explicit manner.

- **Use Manipulatives (and Tools and Technology)** In the early grades manipulatives may include counters and blocks that enable students to carry out a mathematical operation, literally with their hands, and actually see the concrete results of that operation. At more advanced levels, measuring tools such as rulers and protractors and technological aids such as calculators and computers will be used. The effectiveness of these tools will be enhanced if they are used within the context of a project that students are intrinsically motivated to initiate and complete.

• **Use Small-Group Interactions and Peer Questioning** Working either as a whole class or in heterogeneous groups or pairs, students can engage in real-life or simulated projects that require application of a variety of mathematical skills. Díaz-Rico and Weed (2002) give as an example a project in which students are told that the classroom needs to be re-carpeted. They first estimate the area and then check their estimates with measuring tools. Working in groups, students could also calculate the potential cost of floor coverings using prices for various types of floor coverings obtained from local catalogues or advertisements.

• **Use Pictures, Real Objects, and Graphic Organizers** We commonly hear the expression "A picture is worth a thousand words." There is a lot of truth to this when it comes to teaching academic content. Visuals enable students to "see" the basic concept we are trying to teach much more effectively than if we rely only on words. Once students grasp the concept, they are much more likely to be able to figure out the meanings of the words we use to talk about it. Among the visuals we can use in presenting math content are these: *pictures/photographs, real objects, graphic organizers, drawings on overhead projectors,* and *blackline masters.* Graphic organizers are particularly useful because they can be used not only by teachers to present concepts but also by students to take notes, organize their ideas in logical categories, and summarize the results of group brainstorming on particular issues. Some graphic organizers that are useful for teaching math are *Venn diagrams; pie and bar graphs; K-W-L charts* (What we know, what we want to know, and what we have learned; *T-charts* (e.g., for comparing and contrasting); *Problem and Solution charts; Main Idea and Details charts; Cause and Effect charts; Sequence charts;* and *Time Lines.*

• **Clarify Language (Paraphrase Ideas, Enunciate Clearly, Adjust Speech Rate, and Simplify Sentences)** This category includes a variety of strategies and language-oriented activities that clarify the meanings of new words and concepts. Teachers can modify their language to students by *paraphrasing ideas and by explaining new concepts and words.* They can explain new words by providing synonyms, antonyms, and definitions either in English or in the home language of students, if they know it. Important vocabulary can be repeated and recycled as part of the paraphrasing of ideas. Teachers should speak in a natural rhythm, but enunciate clearly and adjust their speech to a rate that ESL students will find easier to understand. Meaning can also be communicated and/or reinforced through gestures, body language, and demonstrations.

Because of their common roots in Latin and Greek, much of the technical math vocabulary in English has cognates in Romance languages, such as Spanish (e.g., *addition—adición*). Students who know these languages can be encouraged to make these cross-linguistic linkages as a means of reinforcing the concept. Bilingual and English-only dictionaries can also be useful tools for language clarification, particularly for intermediate-grade students.

- **Use Total Physical Response, Gestures, and Pantomime** For beginning ESL Students, *Total Physical Response,* activities wherein students act out commands, can be highly effective. Math calculations can be embedded in the commands that students act out. For example, students can progress from fully acting out the command "Take 5 steps forward and then 2 steps backward" to calculating in their heads that they need take only 3 steps forward to reach the destination. Additionally, the meanings of individual words can be demonstrated through *gestures* and *pantomime.*

- **Give Frequent Feedback and Expand Student Responses** *Giving frequent feedback* means responding positively and naturally to all forms of responses. Teachers can let their students know how they are doing by responding to both their words and their actions. Teachers can also assess their students' understanding by asking them to give examples, or by asking them how they would explain a concept or idea to someone else. *Expanding student responses* often means using polar (either/or) questions with students who are just beginning to produce oral English and "wh" (who, what, when, where, why) questions with students who are more fluent. Teachers can easily, and casually, expand their students' one- and two-word answers into complete sentences ("Yes, a triangle does have three sides") and respond to grammatically incorrect answers by recasting them using standard English syntax (Student: "I gotted 4 tens and 1 one"; Teacher: "That's right, you have 4 tens and 1 one").

Extend Language

A systematic focus on and exploration of language is essential if students are to develop knowledge of the specific vocabulary and discursive patterns within the genre of mathematical language. As noted above, investigation of the language of mathematics can also develop in students a curiosity about language and deepen their understanding of how words work. Three strategies for extending students' knowledge of the language of mathematics are outlined below.

A. Creating mathematical language banks

Students can systematically collect the meanings of words and phrases they encounter in mathematical texts in a personal or group *language bank.* Ideally, the language bank would be created in a series of files within the classroom computer but it can also be done with paper and pencil in a class notebook.

Paradoxically, the complexity of mathematical language provides some important opportunities for language exploration. As mentioned above, a large percentage of the less frequent academic and technical vocabulary of English derives from Latin and Greek roots. One implication of this is that word formation follows some very predictable patterns. These patterns are similar in English and Spanish.

When students know some of the rules or conventions of how academic words are formed, it gives them an edge in extending their vocabulary. It helps them figure out not only the meanings of individual words but also how to form different parts of speech from those words.

A central aspect of academic language is *nominalization.* This refers to the process whereby abstract nouns are formed from verbs and adjectives. Take, for example, four common verbs that occur in the math curriculum: *multiply, divide, measure,* and *equal.* The word families (excluding verb forms and plurals) for each of these words are presented below.

Verb	Noun	Adjective
multiply	multiplication multiple multiplicity	multiple
divide	division dividend	divisive divided
measure	measure measurement	measured
equal equalize	equality equal equalizer	equal equitable

We see in these four word families, several common ways in which the English language forms nouns from verbs. One pattern is to add the suffix *-tion* or *-ion* to the verb form as in *multiplication, division,* and many other mathematical terms, such as *estimation, notation,* and *operation.* Another pattern is to add the suffix *-ment* as in *measurement,* while a third pattern is to add the suffix *-ity* or *-ty* as in *equality, capacity, property,* and *probability.* When we demystify how this academic language works, students are more likely to recognize parts of speech in their reading of complex texts across the curriculum and to become more adept at inferring meaning from context. For example, when a student recognizes that *acceleration* is a noun (rather than a verb or an adjective), he or she is one step closer to understanding the meaning of the term in the context of a particular sentence or text.

Students can be encouraged to use dictionaries (in both English and their L1, when available) to explore the more subtle meanings of these mathematical words. For example, students could be asked to work in pairs or small groups to think through the differences in meaning between the verbs *equal* and *equalize;* among the nouns *equality, equal,* and *equalizer;* and between the adjectives *equal* and *equitable.*

This nominalization process also permits us to think in terms of abstract realities or states and to use higher-level cognitive functions that require uses of language very different from the conversational or "playground" language that we acquire in everyday situations. This point is made clearly by Pauline Gibbons:

> The playground situation does not normally offer children the opportunity to use such language as: *if we increase the angle by 5 degrees, we could cut the circumference into equal parts.* Nor does it normally require the language associated with the higher-order thinking skills, such as hypothesizing, evaluating, inferring, generalizing, predicting, or classifying. Yet these are the language functions which are related to learning and the development of cognition; they occur in all areas of the curriculum, and without them a child's potential in academic areas cannot be realized (1991, p. 3).

Gibbons goes on to point out that explicit modeling of academic language is particularly important in schools with large numbers of ESL students:

> In such a school it is very easy to fall into the habit of constantly simplifying our language because we expect not to be understood. But if we only ever use basic language such as *put in* or *take out* or *go faster,* some children will not have any opportunity to learn other ways of expressing these ideas, such as *insert* or *remove* or *accelerate.* And these are the words that are needed to refer to the general concepts related to the ideas, such as *removal, insertion,* and *acceleration* (1991, p. 18).

In short, when students know some of the rules or conventions of how academic words are formed, it gives them an edge in extending their vocabulary. It helps them figure out not only the meanings of individual words but also how to form different parts of speech from these words. One way of organizing students' language detective work in mathematics is to focus separately on *meaning, form,* and *use.* Working in pairs or small groups, students can be encouraged to collect and explore one mathematics word per day, focusing on one or more of these three categories.

- **Focus on Meaning** Categories that can be explored within a Focus on Meaning include *Mathematical meaning; Everyday meaning; Meaning in other subject areas; L1 equivalents; Related words in L1 (cognates); Synonyms; Antonyms; Homonyms; Meaning of prefix; Meaning of root;* and *Meaning of suffix.* Not all of these categories will be relevant for every word, but considered together they provide a map of directions that an exploration of meaning might pursue. Take a possible exploration of the word *subtract:*

Mathematical meaning:	take one number or quantity from another (or compare two numbers or quantities)
L1 equivalent (Spanish):	restar, sustraer
Synonym:	deduct
Antonym:	add
Meaning of prefix:	under or away
Meaning of root:	from the Latin for "pull"

- **Focus on Form** Most of the root words in mathematics that come from Latin and Greek form not just one part of speech; we can make nouns, verbs, and adjectives from many of these root words. If we know the typical patterns for forming nouns and adjectives from root verbs, we can recognize these parts of speech when they appear in text. The implications for expanding students' vocabulary are clear: rather than learning just one word in isolation, students are enabled to learn entire *word families,* a process that can dramatically expand their working vocabulary.

  Categories that can be explored within a Focus on Form include *Word family and grammatical patterns; Words with the same prefix; Words with the same root;* and *Words with the same suffix.* Consider again the word *subtract:*

Word family/ *grammatical patterns:*	subtract, subtracts, subtracted, subtracting (verb forms)
	subtraction, subtractions (noun forms)
Words with same prefix:	substitute, subtotal, suburban, subway
Words with same root:	tractor, traction

- **Focus on Use** Students can explore the range of uses of particular words through brainstorming as a class or small group; looking words up in dictionaries, encyclopedias, or thesauri; or asking parents or other adults outside of school. Categories that can be explored within a Focus on Use include *General uses; Idioms; Metaphorical uses; Proverbs; Advertisements; Puns;* and *Jokes.* For the word *subtract,* most students will not find much that will fall within these categories other than the category of *general uses.* However, with some of the more frequent words in mathematical discourse that derive from the Anglo-Saxon lexicon of English rather than the Greek/Latin lexicon, many of these other categories will yield a multitude of examples. Consider the multiple meanings and figurative uses of words such as *great* (as in "greater than"), *big,* and *double* that students might explore.

  In short, when students explore the language of mathematics by collecting specimens of mathematical language in a systematic and cumulative way, they expand not only their understanding of mathematical terms and concepts but also their knowledge of how the English language works (e.g., the fact that abstract nouns are often formed in English by adding the suffix *-tion* to the verb). The development of language awareness in this way will benefit students' reading comprehension and writing ability across the curriculum.

B. Taking ownership of mathematical language by means of "reporting back"

If students are to take ownership of mathematical language, we must provide ample opportunities and encouragement for them to use this language for authentic purposes in the classroom. In the absence of active use of the language, students' grasp of the mathematical register is likely to remain shallow and passive.

Researchers (e.g., Swain, 1997) have noted three ways in which L2 acquisition is stimulated by active use of the language:

- Students must try to figure out sophisticated aspects of the target language in order to express what they want to communicate.

- It highlights to both students and teachers the aspects of language the students still find troublesome.

- It provides teachers with the opportunity to provide corrective feedback to build language awareness and help students figure out how the language works.

- **Have Students Report Back Orally and in Writing** One example of how this process operates in the teaching of content areas such as mathematics is provided by Gibbons (1991). She emphasizes the importance of *reporting back* as a strategy for promoting academic language development. For example, after a concrete, hands-on group experience or project, students are asked to report back to the class orally about what they did and observed and then to write about it. As students progress from concrete, hands-on experience to more abstract oral and written language use, they must include sufficient information within the language itself for the meaning to be understood by those who did not share in the original experience. She notes that

> while hands-on experiences are a very valuable starting point for language development, they do not, on their own, offer children adequate opportunities to develop the more 'context-free' language associated with reading and writing.... [A] reporting-back situation is a bridge into the more formal demands of literacy. It allows children to try out in speech—in a realistic and authentic situation—the sort of language they meet in books and which they need to develop in their writing. Where children's own language background has not led to this extension of oral language, it becomes even more important for the classroom to provide such opportunities (1991, p. 31).

In short, students become more aware of the cognitive processes and strategies they use to solve math problems, and they are enabled to take ownership of the language that reflects and facilitates these cognitive processes, when the curriculum provides extensive opportunities for them to explain orally and in written form what they did and how they did it.

C. Mastering the language of mathematical assessment

- **Have Students Create Test Items** High-stakes testing has become a fact of life in classrooms across the United States, and consequently a large majority of curriculum materials include not only formative assessment integrated within the curriculum unit but also practice oriented to performance on state-wide standardized tests. Consistent with the emphasis on providing opportunities for students to take ownership of the language of mathematics through active use of that language, we can also encourage students to gain insight and control over the language of mathematical assessment. We can do this by having students create their own multiple-choice (or other relevant) tests in mathematics rather than always being on the receiving end of tests that adults have created. The process might work as follows.

In order to familiarize students with the process (and also have some fun in a friendly, competitive context), we can have them work in heterogeneous groups to construct their own tests, initially on topics with which they are familiar or on which they have carried out research. For example, the teacher might explain how multiple-choice items are constructed (e.g., the role of distractors), and each group might construct a set of approximately 5 items on topics such as baseball, popular music, television programs, or popular slang. These items are then pooled and the entire set of items is administered as a test to the entire class. Subsequently, each group might research aspects of a particular content area and construct items based on their research. In the context of math, groups could construct test items that focus on the unit of study (e.g., fractions or decimals) that has just been completed. An incentive system could be instituted such that the groups gain points based on their performance on the pooled test that leads ultimately to some reward.

The rationale for this reversal of roles is that construction of test items is more cognitively challenging (and engaging) than simply responding to test items. In order to come up with items that will be challenging for the other groups, students must know the content of the unit in an active rather than a passive way. The within-group discussion and collaboration in generating the items and distractors is also likely to reinforce both language and content knowledge for all students in the group, but particularly for those students (likely including some ESL students) whose grasp of the content may be fragile.

Within this conception, standardized math tests are viewed as one particular genre of math language. Students should be familiar with the conventions of this genre if their academic worth is to be recognized. In generating multiple-choice test items, students are developing language awareness in the context of a highly challenging (but engaging) cognitive activity.

The same principle can be applied to the creation of other forms of assessment that tap both math and language concepts. For example, teachers could have students create multiple-choice cloze sentences that reflect both everyday and math-specific meanings of mathematical vocabulary.

1. Five _____ six _____ eleven.
2. On the _____ side, my share _____ his.
3. On the _____ side, his share is _____ mine.
4. Numbers less than zero are called _____ numbers.
5. When we multiply by two, we _____ the quantity.

Target Words
plus
double
equals
negative

Conclusion

Mathematics will assume relevance to students and be learned much more effectively when they can relate the content to their prior experience and current interests. In addition to activating students' prior knowledge and building background, we may need to modify our instruction in specific ways to make the content accessible to ESL students who are still in the process of catching up to native speakers in academic English- language proficiency. This catch-up process will typically take at least 5 years, partly because students are catching up to a moving target—native speakers of English are not standing still, waiting for ESL students to bridge the gap. Thus, even ESL students who are relatively fluent in English may require specific support in accessing mathematical concepts and problems expressed in English.

These supports should focus not only on making the mathematics content comprehensible to students but also on extending their awareness of how the language of mathematics works. In this way, students can develop insights about academic language that will bear fruit in other content areas (e.g., reading comprehension in language arts and vocabulary building in social studies). A goal of this process of extending students' command of academic language is to enable them to take ownership of the language of the curriculum and use it for authentic purposes. Thus, they will benefit from opportunities to carry out projects and explain what they did both orally and in written form. As the audience becomes more distant (e.g., in the case of a more formal written report), students are required to use more abstract, explicit, and precise language to communicate their meaning. When we integrate these active uses of language with the mathematics curriculum, students benefit both with respect to mathematics and to language facility.

References

Collier, V. P. and Thomas, W. P. (1999). Making U.S. schools effective for English language learners, Part 1. *TESOL Matters*, 9:4 (August/September), pp. 1 & 6.

Cummins (2001). *Negotiating identities: Education for empowerment in a diverse society.* 2nd edition. Los Angeles: California Association for Bilingual Education.

Díaz-Rico, L. & Weed, K. Z. (2002). *The crosscultural, language, and academic development handbook: A complete K–12 reference guide.* 2nd edition. Boston: Allyn & Bacon.

Gibbons, P. (1991). *Learning to learn in a second language.* Newtown, Australia: Primary English Teaching Association.

Meyer, L. (2000). Barriers to meaningful instruction for English learners. *Theory into Practice*, 34(2), 228–236.

Swain, M. (1997). Collaborative dialogue: Its contribution to second language learning. *Revista Canaria de Estudios Ingleses*, 34, 115–132.

Joining Groups to Add

ACCESS CONTENT

USE WITH LESSON
1-1

Objective Join two groups together to find how many in all.

Materials *(per pair)* 108 each of red and yellow counters

Vocabulary Join, sum, in all

ESL Strategies *Use before* **CHECK** ✓ 🕐 10–15 MIN

Use Manipulatives ➤ Display 8 red counters. **How many red counters do you see?** *(8 counters)* Have children count the counters aloud with you. Then display 4 yellow counters near the red counters. **How many yellow counters do you see?** *(4 counters)* **I can join, or bring together, these red and yellow counters.** Move the yellow counters so that they are next to the red counters. **How many counters do you see in all?** *(12 counters)* Have children count them aloud with you. **8 and 4 is 12 in all. 12 is the sum.** Then display 7 red counters and 2 yellow counters. **How many counters do you see in all?** *(9 counters)* **7 joined with 2 makes 9 in all.** Have children repeat the sentence after you. **What is the number 9 called?** *(The sum)*

Use Small-Group Interactions ➤ Divide the class into pairs. Give each pair 10 red counters and 10 yellow counters. **How many different ways can you join red and yellow counters to make 10 counters in all?** Have children take turns grouping the counters and saying each combination aloud.

Writing Addition Sentences

ACCESS CONTENT

USE WITH LESSON
1-2

Objective Join two groups together and write an addition sentence to tell how many in all.

Materials 2 bags; *(per pair)* 12 two-color counters

Vocabulary Plus, sum, equals, addition sentence

ESL Strategies *Use before* **LEARN** 🕐 10 MIN

Use Demonstration ➤ Display 2 empty bags. **Is there anything in these 2 bags?** *(No)* Ask a child to count out 3 counters and to place them in 1 of the bags. As the child counts, write 3 on the board. Then ask another child to place 4 counters in the other bag while counting them aloud. After the 3, write + 4. Using gestures, relate the counters in the bags to the numbers on the board: **There are 3 counters in this bag. There are 4 counters in this bag.** On the board, add "=" to the number phrase. **How many counters are there in all?** Have a volunteer count the number of counters in both bags. *(7 counters)* Write 7 after the equal sign. Point to the number sentence: **This <u>addition sentence</u> tells us that 3 counters and 4 counters make 7 counters in all. 3 <u>plus</u> 4 <u>equals</u> 7, the <u>sum</u>.**

Use Small-Group ➤ Divide the class into pairs and give each pair 12 two-color counters. Write
Interactions ____ + ____ = 12 on the board. Ask one child in each pair to copy this
incomplete addition sentence onto a piece of paper. Encourage children to
use their counters to help them fill in the blanks. Have each pair complete 2
different addition sentences showing numbers that add to 12.

Problem-Solving Strategy: Write a Number Sentence

USE WITH LESSON 1-3

ACCESS CONTENT; EXTEND LANGUAGE

Objective Solve a story problem by writing an addition sentence.

Vocabulary Altogether

ESL Strategies   *Use before* **LEARN**   ⏱ 10 MIN

Focus on Meaning ➤ Use the everyday meaning of <u>altogether</u> to help children learn the
mathematical meaning of the word. **Listen to this sentence: There are
3 apples altogether in a bag. What does *altogether* mean?** *(In all)* **When
you add things, you are looking for how many things there are altogether.**

Use Pictures ➤ Write the following story on the board, using simple pictures to illustrate:

There are 3 puppies playing.

5 more puppies join them.

How many puppies are playing altogether?

Ask a volunteer to write the addition sentence on the board. *(3 + 5 = 8)*

Have Students ➤ Divide the class into pairs. Have each child draw a picture story on a piece of
Create Test Items paper and have partners exchange pictures. Then have each student write an
addition sentence for his or her partner's picture. Invite volunteers to share
their picture stories and addition sentences with the class.

Taking Away to Subtract

ACCESS CONTENT; EXTEND LANGUAGE

Objective Take away a number of objects from a group and count to find how many are left.

Materials Color tiles

Vocabulary Take away, subtract

ESL Strategies   *Use before* **LEARN**   ⏱ 10 MIN

Use Demonstration ➤ Display 6 tiles of the same color. **How many tiles do you see?** *(6 tiles)* Count the tiles aloud with children and write the number 6 on the board. **I am going to <u>take away</u> 4 tiles.** Take away 4 tiles. **How many tiles do you see now?** *(2 tiles)* **When I take away things from a group, I <u>subtract</u>. I started with 6 tiles. How many tiles did I subtract?** *(4 tiles)*

Paraphrase Ideas ➤ **When you take away things from a group, you can find how many things are left in the group.** Write "5 take away 3 is 2" on the board. Read the sentence aloud with children. Hold up 5 tiles. **I have 5 tiles. Now I am going to take away 3 of them.** Take away 3 tiles. **How many tiles do I have left?** *(2 tiles)* Point to the appropriate numbers in the sentence on the board as you repeat: **When you take away, or subtract, 3 from 5, 2 are left.**

Have Students Report Back Orally ➤ Have children volunteer to give their own demonstrations using the color tiles. They should include the words *take away* and *subtract* in their explanations.

Comparing to Find How Many More

ACTIVATE PRIOR KNOWLEDGE/BUILD BACKGROUND; ACCESS CONTENT

Objective Compare two groups to find out how many more or how many fewer.

Materials 7 red and 5 yellow tiles

Vocabulary More, compare

ESL Strategies   *Use before* **LEARN**   ⏱ 10 MIN

Connect to Prior Knowledge of Math ➤ Display 7 red tiles and 5 yellow tiles. **How many red tiles are there?** *(7 tiles)* Write "There are 7 red tiles" on the board. **How many yellow tiles are there?** *(5 tiles)* Write "There are 5 yellow tiles" below the other sentence on the board.

Let us <u>compare</u> the number of red tiles and the number of yellow tiles. Have them count the tiles, alternating between the two colors in this way: One, one; two, two; . . . five, five; six; seven. **Are there <u>more</u> red tiles or yellow tiles?** *(Red tiles)* Recount the red tiles that do not have a matching yellow tile: One, two. **How many more red tiles are there?** *(2 tiles)* Write "There are 2 more red tiles" on the board below the other sentences.

Paraphrase Ideas ➤ **What did we do to find out how many more red tiles there are than yellow tiles?** *(We compared them.)* **When we compare two groups that are not the same, we can subtract.**

Writing Subtraction Sentences

USE WITH LESSON 1-6

EXTEND LANGUAGE; ACCESS CONTENT

Objective Write subtraction sentences to solve both separation and comparison problems.

Materials Bag; 9 counters

Vocabulary Subtraction sentence, difference

ESL Strategies | *Use before* **LEARN**

⏱ 10 MIN

Focus on Meaning ➤ Use the everyday meaning of *difference* to help children learn the mathematical meaning of the word. Help children recognize that the root of the word is *differ*, or "to be unlike." Have children find and name things in the classroom that are different from one another. *(Sample responses: a pen and a pencil, a desk and a chair)*

Use Manipulatives ➤ Put 9 counters in a bag. **How many counters are in the bag?** *(9 counters)* Ask a child to count them. Write the number on the board. **There are 9 counters in the bag. I am going to subtract 3 counters.** Remove 3 counters and write − 3 = on the board after the number 9. Point to the subtraction sentence. **This subtraction sentence tells us about the number of counters. There were 9 counters in the bag, but I subtracted 3 of them. The number of counters that are left in the bag is the difference. How many counters are left?** *(6 counters)* Write 6 after the equal sign. **6 is the difference between 9 and 3.**

Problem-Solving Skill: Choose an Operation

USE WITH LESSON 1-7

ACTIVATE PRIOR KNOWLEDGE/BUILD BACKGROUND

Objective Solve problems by choosing addition or subtraction.

Materials Counters or color tiles; *(per child)* "+" and "−" card

Vocabulary Addition

Use before `LEARN` ⏱ 15 MIN

Connect to Prior ➤
Knowledge of
Math

Distribute "+" and "−" cards. Write a plus sign on the board. Have children hold up the "+" card and ask them what it means. *(Putting things together; joining or adding)* Write the word "addition" on the board. **When you put things together, you are doing addition.** Have children hold up the "−" card and ask them what it means. *(Taking things away; subtracting)* Write the word "subtraction" on the board. **When you take things away or find a difference, you are doing subtraction.**

Write the following problems on the board and read them aloud.

5 birds are sitting in a tree. 2 birds fly away. How many birds are still sitting in the tree? *(3 birds)*

4 children are playing catch. 4 children join them. How many children are playing catch? *(8 children)*

There are 8 pencils on the desk. The teacher takes 6 of them. How many pencils are left on the desk? *(2 pencils)*

For each problem, have children hold up the appropriate symbol card to show whether the problem is an addition or a subtraction problem. For each problem, ask, **What numbers do you add (or subtract)?** Write the numbers on the board. Have children solve the problems. If children have difficulty with a problem, demonstrate it with counters or color tiles.

Adding in Any Order

USE WITH LESSON **1-8**

ACTIVATE PRIOR KNOWLEDGE/BUILD BACKGROUND; EXTEND LANGUAGE

Objective Use the commutative property to find sums.

Materials 8 pencils

Vocabulary Related facts

ESL Strategies

Use before `CHECK ✓` ⏱ 10–15 MIN

Connect to Prior ➤
Knowledge of
Math

Ask two volunteers to come forward and stand next to each other facing the class. Give the first child 6 pencils and the second child 2 pencils. Have the first child hold up the 6 pencils. **How many pencils does (Child A) have?** *(6 pencils)* Write 6 on the board. Then have the second child hold up the 2 pencils. **How many pencils does (Child B) have?** *(2 pencils)* Write 2 on the board next to 6. As you point to the board and gesture to the pencils that each child is holding up, ask, **How many pencils are there altogether?** *(8 pencils)* **6 plus 2 equals 8.** Write the addition sentence $6 + 2 = 8$ on the board.

Have the two children switch places. Repeat the steps above. Write the numbers 2 and 6 on the board after the class has given you the correct answers. **How many pencils are there altogether?** *(8 pencils)* **2 plus 6 equals 8.** Write the addition sentence $2 + 6 = 8$ under $6 + 2 = 8$ so children can compare the addition sentences. **When (Child A) and (Child B) switched places, did the sum change?** *(No)* **The sums are the same when two numbers are added in a different order. We call these addition sentences** <u>related facts</u>.

Focus on Meaning ➤ **We can use the word** *related* **in different ways. Are you related to your mother and father?** *(Yes)* **Are you related to the child next to you?** *(Preferable answer: No)* **What does it mean when two people are related?** *(Responses will vary.)*

Ways to Make 10

USE WITH LESSON 1-9

ACCESS CONTENT

Objective Recognize facts that have sums of 10.

ESL Strategies **Use before** **LEARN** ⏱ 10–15 MIN

Use Total ➤ Physical Response

Have 10 children come to the front of the room, some to the left and some to the right. The groups do not have to be equal. **How many children are there altogether?** *(10 children)* Write ____ + ____ = 10 on the board. **How many are on the left?** Have a volunteer write the first addend. **How many are on the right?** Ask another volunteer to write the second addend. **These numbers are addends. Does the sum of the addends equal 10?** *(Yes)*

Ask some of the 10 children to face the front of the room and others to face the back. The groups do not have to be equal. **How many children are there altogether?** *(10 children)* Write ____ + ____ = 10 on the board beneath the first example. **How many children are facing the front of the room?** Have a volunteer write the first addend. **How many are facing the back of the room?** Ask another volunteer to write the second addend. **Does the sum of the addends equal 10?** *(Yes)*

Expand Student ➤ Responses

Have a volunteer select some of the children to face in the opposite direction. Then have the volunteer go to the board to write the new addition sentence. Continue the activity, finding as many different number sentences equaling 10 as the children can find. *(0 + 10; 1 + 9; 2 + 8; 3 + 7; 4 + 6; 5 + 5; 6 + 4; 7 + 3; 8 + 2; 9 + 1; 10 + 0)* Discuss with the class the addition sentences that they did not find.

Fact Families

ACTIVATE PRIOR KNOWLEDGE/BUILD BACKGROUND; ACCESS CONTENT

Objective Write the addition and subtraction sentences that make up a fact family.

Vocabulary Fact family

ESL Strategies | *Use before* **LEARN** | 🕐 10–15 MIN

Connect to Prior Knowledge of Math ➤ Ask 4 volunteers to come to the front of the class. Arrange them so that 3 children stand to your right and 1 stands to your left. Starting with the 3 children on your right, have the class count all of the volunteers along with you: **1, 2, 3, 4.** Write $3 + 1 = 4$ on the board. Use gestures to show the relationship between each number and the children as you say, **These two groups show the addition fact 3 plus 1 equals 4.** Have children repeat the addition fact along with you. As they do, trace the number sentence with your finger. Then reverse the position of the children so that 1 child stands to your right and 3 children stand to your left. **What addition fact do these two groups show us now?** *(1 + 3 = 4)* Have a child say the number sentence aloud and write it beneath the first fact.

Expand Student Responses ➤ Have the 4 children stand together. **How many children are there altogether?** *(4 children)* Have 1 child move away from the group. **If we take away 1, how many children are left?** *(3 children)* Write $4 - 1 = 3$ on the board beneath the 2 addition facts. Repeat the process to demonstrate the subtraction fact $4 - 3 = 1$. Draw a square to enclose the set of 4 number sentences. **These 4 number facts make up a fact family. Each number fact in a fact family uses the same 3 numbers.** Write "fact family" above the square, and have children read all 4 facts aloud.

Use Small-Group Interactions ➤ Divide the class into pairs. Write the numbers 5, 7, and 12 on the board. Ask each pair to write down all the number facts in the fact family. *(5 + 7 = 12; 7 + 5 = 12; 12 − 5 = 7; 12 − 7 = 5)*

Finding the Missing Part

ACCESS CONTENT; ACTIVATE PRIOR KNOWLEDGE/BUILD BACKGROUND

Objective Use counters to find the missing addend in an addition sentence.

Materials Two-color counters

ESL Strategies | *Use before* **LEARN** | 🕐 10 MIN

Use Demonstration ➤ Have 8 children stand in front of the class. **How many children are in front of the class?** *(8 children)* **I want 12 children altogether to stand in front of the class.** Write $8 + \_\_\_\_ = 12$ on the board. **We need to figure out how many more children must come up to the front to make 12 children.**

Ask 2 children to come forward and stand a few feet away from the 8 children already in front of the class. **Let us see if 2 more children will make 12 children altogether.** With the class, count aloud the number of children in front of the class, saying: **1, 2, 3 . . . 9, 10. How many children are there now?** *(10 children)* **We still do not have 12 children.** Repeat the process, asking 2 more children to come forward. Complete the number sentence on the board and read it aloud with children: **8 + 4 = 12.**

Use Role Playing ➢ Tell children that they are going to plan how to make a vegetable salad together. On the board, write "11 carrots." **We need 11 carrots for our salad.** Place 4 counters on a desk. **We only have 4 carrots.** Write 4 + _____ = 11 on the board. **How many more carrots do we need to make 11 carrots?** *(7 carrots)* Have a child role-play the part of a worker at a store. Role-play the customer and say to the child, **I only have 4 carrots. I need 11 in all. May I have some more carrots, please?** Have the child first count the number of counters on the desk: "1, 2, 3, 4." He or she then counts out enough counters for you to make 11: "5, 6, 7 … 11." The child says how many more carrots he or she gave you: "I gave you 7 more carrots." Complete the number sentence and have children read it aloud with you. Continue the activity, making number sentences for other salad ingredients, such as tomatoes, onions, and peppers. For each vegetable, have different children act as the worker and the customer in a store.

Problem-Solving Applications: Frogs and Toads

EXTEND LANGUAGE

Objective Review and apply key concepts, skills, and strategies learned in this and previous chapters.

ESL Strategies

Use before **LEARN**

⏱ 10 MIN

Have Students ➤ Report Back in Writing

Divide the class into pairs. Have them read aloud the *Writing in Math* stories they wrote in their journals about toads and mealworms. Then have them write any number sentences they found in each others' stories in their journal.

Have children identify addition and subtraction ideas that they learned from this chapter in the number sentences. Ask for a volunteer who has identified a comparison in his or her partner's story to come forward and write the number sentence on the board. Ask the other children, **Can you compare these things? Why do you think so?**

After a short discussion to clarify any questions about comparison, continue the process, this time asking for a volunteer who has identified a fact family. Go through the same process. Continue in this manner, covering adding in any order, ways to make 10, finding the missing part, and any other lesson from this chapter.

Counting On

USE WITH LESSON 2-1

ACTIVATE PRIOR KNOWLEDGE/BUILD BACKGROUND; EXTEND LANGUAGE

Objective Count on to add 1, 2, or 3 to another number.

Vocabulary Count on, add, sum

ESL Strategies | **Use before** LEARN | ⏱ 10 MIN

Focus on Use ➤ Write "count on" on the board. Have children read the words with you. **The word *on* in count on means more. So what does *count on* mean?** *(To count more)*

Connect to Prior Knowledge of Math ➤ **Let us count to five: 1, 2, 3, 4, 5.** Write each number on the board as the children count. **Now let us add one more: 1, 2, 3, 4, 5, 6. When you count on one more from 5, what number do you get?** *(6)* **In other words, when you add 5 and 1, you get a sum of 6.** Write the number 6 on the board. Repeat the process with counting on to 7. **When you count on two more from 5, what number do you get?** *(7)* **So when you add 5 and 2, what is the sum?** *(7)*

Repeat the process to count on to 8.

Doubles Fact to 18

USE WITH LESSON 2-2

ACCESS CONTENT

Objective Recognize doubles as a strategy for remembering sums.

Materials 8 pencils; 2 cups; *(per pair)* 18 connecting cubes

Vocabulary Addition fact, addend, doubles fact

ESL Strategies | **Use before** CHECK ✓ | ⏱ 10 MIN

Use Real Objects ➤ Count out 3 pencils and put them in one cup. **How many pencils are in this cup?** *(3 pencils)* Write 3 on the board. Count out 3 more pencils and put them in the other cup. **How many pencils are in this cup?** *(3 pencils)* Write 3 on the board next to the 3 already on the board (leave space for a plus sign). **Let us count on to find the sum: 1, 2, 3 . . . 4, 5, 6. How many pencils are there in all?** *(6 pencils)* The sum of 3 and 3 is 6. Write out the addition sentence, adding a 6, a plus sign, and a equal symbol to the numbers already on the board. **3 + 3 = 6 is an addition fact. Since the addends are the same, we can also call it a doubles fact.**

Add 2 more pencils, one to each cup, and repeat the process for 4 + 4 = 8. **What do you notice about this addition fact?** *(The addends are the same.)* **What kind of addition fact is it?** *(A doubles fact)*

| Use Small-Group Interactions | ➤ | Divide the class into pairs. Give each pair 18 connecting cubes. Write 6, 7, and 8 on the board. Have Partner A show the double of the first number, 6, with cubes. Then have Partner B write the corresponding doubles fact on paper. *(6 + 6 = 12)* Then have children switch roles so that Partner B shows doubles with cubes, and Partner A writes the corresponding doubles fact for 7. *(7 + 7 = 14)* Then have both children work with the cubes to find the doubles fact for 8. *(8 + 8 = 16)* |

Doubles Plus 1

USE WITH LESSON 2-3

ACTIVATE PRIOR KNOWLEDGE/BUILD BACKGROUND; ACCESS CONTENT

Objective Use doubles facts to learn doubles-plus-1 facts.

Materials 8 pencils; 2 cups; *(per pair)* 18 connecting cubes

ESL Strategies ⌐ *Use before* **CHECK ✓**   ⏱ 10 MIN

Connect to Prior Knowledge of Math	➤	Show children 2 cups and 6 pencils. Put 3 pencils in each cup. Point to the first cup. **How many pencils are in this cup?** *(3 pencils)* Point to the second cup. **How many pencils are in this cup?** *(3 pencils)* **How many pencils are there in all?** *(6 pencils)* Write 3 + 3 = 6 on the board. **What fact tells you how many pencils there are in all?** *(A doubles fact)*
		Put another pencil into the second cup. Write 3 + 4 = ___ under the doubles fact on the board. **What is 3 + 4?** *(7)* **How does using doubles help you know this?** *(3 + 3 = 6. 1 more is 7.)* Have a child come forward and write the sum to complete the addition fact. *(3 + 4 = 7)* **What other addition fact can you write for this sum?** *(4 + 3 = 7)* Have another child come forward and write the addition fact under the first two.
Use Small-Group Interactions	➤	Group children into pairs. Give each pair 18 connecting cubes. Write 6, 7, and 8 on the board. Have children use the cubes to show the double of the first number, 6, and write the corresponding doubles fact on paper. *(6 + 6 = 12)* Then have them add 1 cube to their cube train and write the addition fact, using doubles plus 1. *(7 + 6 = 13)* Repeat the process for 7 and 8. Ask volunteers to show one of the doubles plus 1 facts that they found. *(7 + 8 = 15 or 8 + 9 = 17)*

Using Strategies to Add Three Numbers

ACTIVATE PRIOR KNOWLEDGE/BUILD BACKGROUND

Objective Find the sum of three addends.

Materials 2 envelopes; index cards numbered 0–9

ESL Strategies

Use before LEARN

⏱ 10–15 MIN

Connect to Prior Knowledge of Math ➤ Write the numbers 0 through 6 on individual index cards and place them in one envelope. Write the numbers 7, 8, and 9 on individual index cards and place them in the other envelope.

Ask three children to come forward. Have the first child randomly pick a card from the first envelope, hold up the card, and say the number. Write the number on the board, and have the child replace the card in the envelope. Ask the second child to pick a card randomly from the second envelope, hold up the card, and say the number. Write the number on the board, below the other number, and have the child replace the card. **When you add these two numbers together, what is the sum?** *(Answers will vary.)* Ask the third child to pick a number from the first envelope, hold it up, and say the number. Write the third number below the first two and add a plus sign. **When you add these three addends together, what is the sum?** *(Answers will vary.)*

Continue having different children randomly pick three numbers from the envelopes. Guide children through the process of adding them. Ask children whether or not a strategy that they know, such as counting on, doubles facts, or doubles plus 1, will make the addition easier. Ask them to explain their strategy.

Making 10 to Add 9

ACCESS CONTENT

Objective Find sums by making a 10 when adding a 9.

Materials *(per child)* 12 counters; 2 Workmat 3s

ESL Strategies **Use before** LEARN

⏱ 10 MIN

Use Manipulatives ➤ Give each child 12 counters and two ten-frame workmats. Have each child place 9 counters on one of the ten-frame workmats by first filling the top row with 5 counters and then filling the first four squares in the bottom row. **How many more counters do you need on your workmat to make 10?** *(1 more)* Have children add one more counter to their ten-frames. Write $9 + 1 = 10$ on the board. Have a volunteer read the addition fact aloud. **How many counters do you have left?** *(2 counters)* Then ask each child to place the remaining two counters in the other ten-frame. **Let us count on to find the**

new sum: 10, 11, 12. How many counters do you have in all? *(12 counters)*
Have a volunteer write the corresponding addition fact under the first
addition fact on the board. *(10 + 2 = 12)*

Demonstrate how to make 10 to add 9 by writing $9 + 1 + 2 = 12$ on the board.
Explain that when 9 is one of the addends, you can add 1 to make 10 and then
count on to find the sum. Invite children to read the new addition fact with you.

Making 10 to Add 7 or 8

USE WITH LESSON 2-6

ACCESS CONTENT

Objective Find sums by making a 10 when adding a 7 or an 8.

Materials 13 pencils; *(per pair)* 14 counters; 2 Workmat 3s

ESL Strategies

Use before **LEARN**

⏱ 10 MIN

Use Manipulatives ➤ Divide the class into pairs. Distribute 14 counters and 2 ten-frame workmats
to each pair. Display a group of 7 pencils and a group of 6 pencils. Count the
group of 7 pencils aloud and have one partner gather 7 counters. Then count
the 6 pencils aloud and have the other partner gather 6 counters. Count all the
pencils with children and write $7 + 6 = 13$ on the board. Have a volunteer
read the addition fact aloud.

**You can show this addition fact with your counters. Put the 7 counters
on your workmat.** Point to the group of 7 pencils. **How many more pencils
do you need to make 10?** *(3 pencils)* Move 3 pencils from the group of 6
pencils to the group of 7. **How many more counters do you need to make
10?** *(3 counters)* Have each pair add 3 counters to their ten-frame. Count the
group of 10 pencils and the group of 10 counters with children.

How many counters do you have left? *(3 counters)* Count on with children
to see how many there are in all: **10 . . . 11, 12, 13.** Write $7 + 3 + 3 = 13$ on
the board. Explain that when 7 is one of the addends, you can add 3 to make
10, and then count on to find the sum. Invite children to read the new
addition fact with you.

Problem-Solving Strategy: Write a Number Sentence

EXTEND LANGUAGE; ACTIVATE PRIOR KNOWLEDGE/BUILD BACKGROUND

Objective Solve problems by writing number sentences.

Vocabulary Number sentence

ESL Strategies

Use before **LEARN**   ⏱ 5–10 MIN

Focus on Meaning ➤ **When you talk, you put words together into sentences. Sentences let you tell stories. Sentences let you ask questions. How else can you use sentences?** *(Sample responses: To tell what you think, to answer questions, to tell what you know)*

In the same way, in math you use numbers to make sentences. How can you use <u>number sentences</u>? *(Sample responses: To ask questions about math, to answer questions about math, to tell math stories)*

What symbols do you use when you write a number sentence? *(Plus sign, minus sign, equal sign)* **What kinds of number sentences have you written?** *(Addition sentences, subtraction sentences)*

Connect to Prior Knowledge of Math ➤ Ask two children to come forward. Have two other children volunteer to read, one at a time, an addition sentence and a subtraction sentence that they wrote in an earlier lesson. Have the first two children write the sentences on the board.

Counting Back

ACTIVATE PRIOR KNOWLEDGE/BUILD BACKGROUND

Objective Use a number line to count back 1 or 2.

Vocabulary Count back, subtract

ESL Strategies

Use before **CHECK** ✓   ⏱ 5–10 MIN

Connect to Prior Knowledge of Math ➤ Draw a number line on the board that shows 0 through 10. **When you count on from a number, which way do you go on the number line?** *(Up, to higher numbers)* Invite a volunteer to come forward. Ask the child to count on 2 from 5 while pointing at the corresponding numbers on the number line. **When you count on, you add. What number sentence did you make when you counted on 2 from 5?** *(5 + 2 = 7)*

When you <u>count back</u> from a number, which way do you go on the number line? *(Back, to lower numbers)* **Now, let us count back 1 from 7.** Point to the corresponding numbers on the number line as the class counts aloud with you: **7, 6. When you count back, you <u>subtract</u>. When we counted back 1 from 7, we found out that 7 − 1 = 6.** Write the subtraction sentence on the board.

Ask a volunteer to come up to the board. Ask the child to count back 2 from 7 on the number line. **What subtraction sentence did you make when you counted back 2 from 7?** *(7 − 2 = 5)*

Thinking Doubles to Subtract

USE WITH LESSON 2-9

ACTIVATE PRIOR KNOWLEDGE/BUILD BACKGROUND; ACCESS CONTENT

Objective Find differences by using doubles facts.

Materials *(per pair)* 8 connecting cubes

ESL Strategies

Use before LEARN

⏱ 10–15 MIN

Connect to Prior Knowledge of Math ➤ Divide the class into pairs. Give each pair a train of 4 connecting cubes. **How many cubes are in your train?** *(4 cubes)* **Break up your train and make 2 smaller trains, each with the same number of cubes. How many cubes are in each train?** *(2 cubes)* Write 2 + 2 = 4 on the board and read the number sentence together with children. **What do you notice about this addition sentence?** *(There are two 2s.)* **How does this relate to the word** *doubles?* *(Doubles are two of the same thing. We added two of the same number.)* Give each pair 2 more cubes and ask them to make 2 trains with the same number of cubes. **How many cubes are in each train?** *(3 cubes)* **What number sentence can you make with your trains?** *(3 + 3 = 6)* Give each pair 2 more cubes and repeat the process with 4 + 4 = 8.

Use Small-Group Interactions ➤ Ask pairs to make a train with the eight cubes. On the board, write 8 − 4 = ____ under 4 + 4 = 8. Point to the numbers in the number sentences. **How are these two number sentences alike?** *(Both use the same numbers.)* Point to the addition fact 4 + 4 = 8. **When you subtract, think about whether or not there is a doubles fact that can help you. If 4 + 4 = 8, what is 8 − 4?** *(4)*

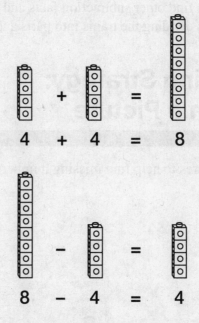

4 + 4 = 8

8 − 4 = 4

Have children demonstrate the subtraction with their cube trains if they have difficulty answering. Have a child complete the subtraction sentence on the board. Then have pairs of children write addition and subtraction facts with doubles for two trains of 2 (2 + 2 = 4, 4 − 2 = 2) and two trains of 3 (3 + 3 = 6, 6 − 3 = 3).

Thinking Addition to Subtract

USE WITH LESSON 2-10

ACCESS CONTENT

Objective Find differences by using addition facts.

Materials *(per pair)* 8 connecting cubes

ESL Strategies   *Use before* **LEARN**   ⏱ 10 MIN

Use Manipulatives ➤ Divide the class into pairs. Give each pair a train of 8 connecting cubes. **How many cubes are in your train?** *(8 cubes)* **Take away 3 cubes. How many cubes are left in your train?** *(5 cubes)* Write 8 − 3 = 5 on the board and have children read this subtraction sentence along with you. **If you add the 3 cubes back to your train, how many cubes will you have in your train?** *(8 cubes)* Write 5 + 3 = 8 on the board. Point to the two number sentences. **How are these two number sentences alike?** *(Both use the same numbers.)* Explain that because 8 − 3 = 5 and 5 + 3 = 8 use the same numbers, children can think of the addition fact to help them solve the subtraction fact.

Use Small-Group Interactions ➤ Have each pair make two trains, one with 2 cubes and the other with 6 cubes. **Suppose you then add your trains together. What addition sentence can you make?** *(2 + 6 = 8)* Have children join their trains to verify the answer. Write the addition sentence on the board. Below it, write 8 − 6 = ___ . **What is 8 − 6?** *(2)* Have pairs use different numbers of cubes (4, 5, 6, and 7) to help them find other subtraction facts and related addition facts. Have children take turns dividing the trains into parts and writing the number sentences.

Problem-Solving Strategy: Use Data from a Picture

USE WITH LESSON 2-11

ACCESS CONTENT

Objective Use data in pictures to help find missing numbers in number sentences.

Use before **CHECK ✓**   ⏱ 10 MIN

Use Pictures ➤ **How far is it from Laketown to River City? We can write a number sentence to find out. Suppose you are standing at the sign. How far are you from Laketown?** *(7 mi)* Draw a number line with the numbers 0 through 20 on the board. Label 0 with "Laketown." **If we start from Laketown, we can count on 7 to find the signpost: 1, 2, . . . 7.** Label 7 with "signpost." Draw an arrow that looks like a semicircle from "Laketown" to "signpost" and write the number 7 to the side of the arrow. **What does the sign tell you about River City?** *(River City is 9 mi from the sign.)* Draw another number line, below the other one, with 0 at "signpost" and extending through 9. **Suppose we start from the signpost. What number do we count on by to find River City?** *(9)* Have the class count aloud with you as you count up the number line. Label 9 "River City." Draw another arrow from "signpost" to "River City" and write the number 9 next to the 7.

Are you adding or subtracting? *(Adding)* Write a plus sign between 7 and 9. **It is 7 miles from Laketown to the sign. It is 9 more miles from the sign to River City. Is this the same as the distance from Laketown to River City?** *(Yes)* Write = ____ after the 9. **Now you have a number sentence that you know how to solve. Let us solve it. How far is it from Laketown to River City?** *(16 mi)* Point out that 9 on the lower number line is at the same place as 16 on the top number line.

Problem-Solving Applications: Baby Birds

USE WITH LESSON
2-12

EXTEND LANGUAGE

Objective Review and apply key concepts, skills, and strategies learned in this and previous chapters.

Use after **LEARN**   ⏱ 15 MIN

Have Students ➤ Divide the class into pairs. Have each child read aloud to his or her partner
Report Back the *Writing in Math* story about flamingos that children wrote in their
in Writing journals. Now ask them to write in their journals any number sentences that they found in each other's stories that helped solve a word problem.

Ask children to look at those number sentences and find some subtraction strategies that they have learned. Ask for a volunteer who has identified a strategy in his or her partner's story to come forward. Have him or her write the number sentence and the identified strategy on the board. Ask the other children: **Do you think that this strategy, or plan, works? How do you know? Can you think of other strategies you can use to solve this problem?** *(Answers will vary by problem.)*

After a short discussion to clarify any questions about subtraction strategies, continue the process. This time ask for a volunteer who has identified a doubles fact. Go through the same procedure. Continue in this way, covering strategies to add three numbers, make 10, and counting back. You can also use concepts from any other lesson from this chapter.

Counting with Tens and Ones

ACCESS CONTENT

USE WITH LESSON 3-1

Objective Count groups of ten, up to 10 tens, and write how many.

Vocabulary Tens, ones

ESL Strategies

Use before **LEARN**

🕐 15 MIN

Use ➤
Demonstration

Have 4 children stand in front of the board, some distance apart, and hold up both hands with all 10 fingers extended. **How many fingers is each child holding up?** *(10 fingers)* Ask children to put down their hands. **How many children are there?** *(4 children)* Have the 4 children hold up their 10 fingers again. Point to each child's hands and say **Here is 1 set of 10 fingers.** Behind each child, write "10 fingers" on the board. **How many <u>tens</u> are there altogether?** *(4 tens)*

Expand Student ➤
Responses

Write the number 34 on the board. Have a volunteer show this number using the fingers of the 4 children at the front. **How many tens are there in all?** *(3 tens)* **How many <u>ones</u> is (Child 4) holding up?** *(4 ones)* Repeat the activity with other numbers.

Using Tens and Ones

ACCESS CONTENT

USE WITH LESSON 3-2

Objective Use groups of tens and ones to show a given two-digit number.

Materials *(per group)* 5 pennies; 10 pennies; narrow 12-inch cardboard strip; tape dispenser

ESL Strategies

Use before **LEARN**

🕐 10 MIN

Use Real Objects ➤

Divide the class into small groups. (There should be no more than 9 groups in all.) Give each group a narrow 12-inch cardboard strip, 10 pennies, and a tape dispenser. Have each group tape the 10 pennies onto the strip, then collect them. Write ___ tens ___ ones on the board.

Hold up 1 cardboard strip. **How many pennies are on this cardboard?** *(10 pennies)* Hold up another. **How many pennies are on this cardboard?** *(10 pennies)* **We have 2 groups of 10 pennies.** Write 2 in the blank before "tens" on the board.

Pick up 5 pennies and count them aloud with the children. **How many pennies do we have?** *(5 pennies)* Write 5 in the blank before "ones" on the board. Hold up the 2 strips of 10 pennies along with the 5 pennies. **How many pennies do we have altogether?** *(2 tens and 5 ones)*

Write 25 on the board. **You know that 2 tens and 5 ones is 25. What did you do to find that we had 25 pennies?** *(First we counted the tens. Then we counted the ones.)* **How was that easier than counting every penny?** *(It is faster to count tens.)* Repeat the activity with other numbers. Invite volunteers to demonstrate other numbers greater than 10 using groups of tens and ones.

Number Words

USE WITH LESSON 3-3

ACCESS CONTENT; EXTEND LANGUAGE

Objective Read and write number words for given numbers.

Materials Index cards

Vocabulary Digit, number word

ESL Strategies

Use before LEARN

⏱ 10 MIN

Use Demonstration ➤ Write the numbers from 0 to 9 on the board. Point to each number in turn and as you do so, have children hold up the corresponding number of fingers. Have children say the numbers aloud with you: **0, 1, 2 . . . 9.**

Focus on Meaning ➤ Write the number word for each <u>digit</u> above the numbers on the board. **We can write each number from 0 to 9 in two ways. We can write the number.** Point to one of the digits. **When we write the number, we call it a digit.** Clearly say the word *digit* again and invite children to repeat after you. **We can also write a word for the number.** Point to the corresponding <u>number word</u>. **We call this a number word. The digit and number word are equal.** Point to the digit 5. **This is the digit 5.** Point to the word *five*. **This is the number word *five*. We can write 5 as a digit, or we can write 5 as a number word.** Invite different volunteers to pronounce each number word as you point to the corresponding digit.

Erase the digits on the board and leave the number words. Write each digit from 0 to 9 on a separate index card. Shuffle them and place them in a stack facedown. Invite a child to come up to the front of the room and choose one of the index cards from the stack. Ask him or her to say the number on the card. Have the child point to the number word on the board that matches the digit. Then have the child replace his or her card facedown on the bottom of the stack. Repeat the activity with other volunteers.

Problem-Solving Strategy:
Make an Organized List

ACCESS CONTENT

Objective Solve a problem by making an organized list.

Materials *(per group)* 10 pennies; cardboard strip; tape dispenser

ESL Strategies   *Use before* **LEARN**   🕐 15 MIN

Use Real Objects ➤ If you did not do so in activity 3-2, give each group a narrow 12" cardboard strip, 10 pennies, and a tape dispenser, and ask each group to tape the pennies in a column down the strip. Collect the strips and stand them in the chalk tray so that they are visible against the board.

Ask two volunteers to come forward. Have one child take 4 of the strips and the other child take 2 of the strips. Stand beside the child with 4 strips and point to the strips one at a time. **Count aloud with me: 10, 20, 30, 40.** Write 40 on the board. Repeat with the child with 2 strips and write 20 to the right of 40. Then add + and = to form the addition problem $40 + 20 = $ ___. Ask one of the volunteers to complete the number sentence. *(60)*

Use Small-Group Interactions ➤ Arrange the class into six groups. Assign each group a number from 0 to 6. Have each group come forward in numerical order, asking one child in each group to hold the number of strips matching the number assigned to their group, and another child to hold the rest. Have a third child write a number sentence, like the one on the board, to show the sum. Have each group come forward and write their number sentence on the board. **What do you see about all these number sentences?** *(They all have a sum of 60.)*

Comparing Numbers

ACCESS CONTENT

Objective Compare numbers using the greater-than, less-than, and equal-to symbols.

Materials 9 cardboard strips of 10 pennies; 9 pennies

Vocabulary Greater than, less than

ESL Strategies   *Use before* **LEARN**   🕐 10 MIN

Use Real Objects ➤ Reuse the strips of pennies from previous activities. Have one child stand in front of the board with 3 strips of pennies plus 2 pennies. **How many pennies does (Child 1) have?** *(32 pennies)* Write 32 on the board above (Child 1's) head. With a space between them, have a second child stand in front of the board with 2 strips of pennies plus 4 pennies. **How many**

pennies does (Child 2) have? *(24 pennies)* Write 24 on the board above (Child 2's) head.

Which place in these numbers tells you which number is more? *(The tens place)* **Look at the tens in both numbers.** Point to 32. **How many tens are in this number?** *(3 tens)* Point to 24. **How many tens are in this number?** *(2 tens)* **Which number has more tens?** *(32)* **So, 32 is more than 24. We can also say that 32 is <u>greater than</u> 24.** Write > on the board between 32 and 24 and point to it. **This symbol, or sign, means greater than.** Read 32 > 24 aloud with the class. Have the two children switch places and repeat the activity for <u>less than</u>. **What do you see about these two symbols? Which way does the point always face?** *(At the smaller number)* **Which way does the open end always face?** *(At the larger number)* Then repeat the process with other numbers and have children write >, <, or = on the board between their classmates.

Finding the Closest Ten

USE WITH LESSON **3-6**

ACTIVATE PRIOR KNOWLEDGE/BUILD BACKGROUND; ACCESS CONTENT

Objective Use a number line to determine the closest ten.

Materials 11 index cards numbered from 10 to 20 in large digits

Vocabulary Closest ten

ESL Strategies

Use before **LEARN**

🕐 10 MIN

Connect to Prior Knowledge of Language ➤ Have 6 children come forward and line up side to side in front of the class. **Who is (Child 2) closer to, (Child 1) or (Child 5)?** *(Child 1)* **Who is (Child 4) closer to, (Child 1) or (Child 6)?** *(Child 6)* **Who is (Child 3) closer to, (Child 1) or (Child 4)?** *(Child 4)* **How did you come up with your answers?** *(Sample answer: There is less space between the children that are closer.)*

Use Total Physical Response ➤ Write each number from 10 through 20 on an index card using large digits. Have 5 more children come forward and line up side to side. Hand out each index card in order so that the first child in line has the card for 10 and the last child has 20. Ask (Child 10) and (Child 20) to raise their cards above their heads. Then ask (Child 18) to raise his or her card and take a step forward. **Who is (Child 18) closer to, (Child 10) or (Child 20)?** *(Child 20)*

Which ten is 18 closer to? *(20)* **20 is the <u>closest ten</u>. How do you know which ten a number is closer to?** *(We can count the numbers between them and compare which number is less.)* Repeat the procedure with several other children in the line.

Before, After, and Between

ACTIVATE PRIOR KNOWLEDGE/BUILD BACKGROUND; ACCESS CONTENT

Objective Identify and write numbers that are one before, one after, or between given numbers.

Materials 16 index cards

Vocabulary Before, after, between

ESL Strategies

Use before **LEARN**　　　　　🕐 10 MIN

Connect to Prior Knowledge of Language ➤ Write the letters A through E, one letter to an index card, and the numbers from 10 through 20 on separate index cards. Arrange the cards in alphabetical and numerical order. **These letters are in the order of the alphabet.** Have children read them aloud with you: **A, B, C, D, E.** Then mix up the order. **Now the letters are not in order.** Have a volunteer put them back in order.

Numbers have an order, too. These numbers are in order from least to greatest. Point to each card in turn and ask children to count aloud with you: **10, 11, 12 . . . 20.** Rearrange the cards so that they are in random order. **Are these numbers in order from least to greatest?** *(No)* Ask for a volunteer to put them back in order.

Use Total Physical Response ➤ Have 3 children stand back-to-front in a line facing the side of the room. **Who is standing <u>before</u> (Child 2) and (Child 3)?** *(Child 1)* **Who is standing <u>after</u> (Child 1) and (Child 2)?** *(Child 3)* **Who is standing <u>between</u> (Child 1) and (Child 3)?** *(Child 2)* Mix the children up and continue to ask *before, after,* and *between* questions. **We can also use the words *before, after,* and *between* to describe numbers. What number comes before 25?** *(24)* **What number comes after 28?** *(29)* **What number comes between 21 and 23?** *(22)* Invite children to ask their classmates similar questions.

Skip Counting on the Hundred Chart

ACTIVATE PRIOR KNOWLEDGE/BUILD BACKGROUND; EXTEND LANGUAGE

Objective Recognize and extend skip-counting patterns.

Vocabulary Pattern

ESL Strategies

Use before **LEARN**　　　　　🕐 10 MIN

Connect to Prior Knowledge of Math ➤ Write 23, 33, 43, 53, 63, 73 on the board. Read the numbers aloud with children. **This is a <u>pattern</u>. We can find new numbers in the pattern by figuring out how the numbers are related to each other. What number comes after 73?** *(83)* **How do you know?** *(The number of tens always goes up by 1. The pattern gets bigger, or increases, by 10.)* Now write 38, 48, ___, 68, 78 on the board. **Here is another pattern. What is the missing**

number? *(58)* **How do you know?** *(The number of tens goes up by 1.* *48 + 10 = 58. The pattern increases by 10.)* **We know that 68 is bigger than the missing number. How can we also use 68 to find the number?** *(Take away, or subtract, 10 from 68. 68 − 10 = 58.)*

Have Students ➤ Divide the class into pairs. Write the number 62 on the board and have each
Report Back pair write it down. **Now write the number that is 1 ten more.** *(72)* **Now**
in Writing **write the number that is 1 ten less.** *(52)* **Write the number that is 3 tens more than 62.** *(92)* Have one pair show the class what they have written.

Write the number 81 on the board and have each pair write it down. **Write the number that is 1 less.** *(80)* **Write the number that is 10 more.** *(91)* Continue with other numbers, asking pairs to increase or decrease each number by tens or by ones.

Even and Odd Numbers

USE WITH LESSON 3-9

ACTIVATE PRIOR KNOWLEDGE/BUILD BACKGROUND; EXTEND LANGUAGE

Objective Identify numbers as odd or even.

Materials *(per child)* 6 connecting cubes

Vocabulary Even, odd

ESL Strategies | *Use before* LEARN

🕙 10 MIN

Connect to Prior ➤ **When you add doubles, you add two addends that are the same.** Write
Knowledge of $3 + 3 =$ ___ on the board. **Use your cubes to show this number sentence.**
Math **Put together 3 cubes and lay them on your desk. Now put together another 3 cubes and lay them next to the first set.** Draw 2 sets of cubes under the digits on the board, so that their ends line up. **What is the sum of this number sentence?** *(6)* **You can match each cube in one of your cube trains with a cube in the other train. When this happens, we say the number is <u>even</u>.**

Focus on Meaning ➤ **Now take away 1 cube from the first train.** Erase 1 of the cubes from the first set and change the number sentence to $2 + 3 =$ ___. **What has changed?** *(The addends are not the same.)* Guide children through the process of matching cubes, as before. **Can you match every cube from the first addend to a cube from the second addend?** *(No)* **What is the sum of this number sentence?** *(5)* **You cannot match the parts of the number 5. When this happens, we say the number is <u>odd</u>.** Invite volunteers to repeat the above activities with different number combinations to show even and odd numbers.

Ordinal Numbers Through Twentieth

USE WITH LESSON 3-10

ACTIVATE PRIOR KNOWLEDGE/BUILD BACKGROUND; EXTEND LANGUAGE

Objective Use ordinals through *twentieth* to identify position.

Vocabulary Ordinal number

ESL Strategies **Use before** LEARN ⏰ 10 MIN

Connect to Prior Knowledge of Language ➤ Write the letters *A* through *J* on the board, the numbers 1 through 10 below them, and the corresponding ordinals from first to tenth below that. Point to A. **This is the letter A, the start of the alphabet. The alphabet is in order—in alphabetical order.** Point to 1. **This is 1, the start of the numbers. The numbers are in numerical order.** Point to *first*. **A and 1 are first in order. What letter comes next?** *(B)* **What number comes next?** *(2)* **B and 2 are next in order.** Point to *second*. **They are second.** Go through all the letters, numbers, and ordinals. Then point to each ordinal and have children say aloud with you: **First, second, third . . . tenth. These are** <u>ordinal numbers</u>.

Focus on Meaning ➤ **You know that letters have an order, and that makes it easier to learn words. You know that numbers have an order. That makes it easier to count. The ordinal numbers are the names that tell us the order numbers come in. Can you think of times when we use ordinal numbers?** *(Sample responses: To follow steps in doing something; to rank things, like the winners in a contest)*

Problem-Solving Skill: Use Data from a Chart

USE WITH LESSON 3-11

ACTIVATE PRIOR KNOWLEDGE/BUILD BACKGROUND

Objective Solve a problem by using clues and data from a chart.

ESL Strategies **Use before** LEARN ⏰ 10 MIN

Connect to Prior Knowledge of Language ➤ **You learned to make an organized list to help solve problems. How did the list help?** *(Sample responses: It helped us see all the ways to do something. It helped us see number patterns.)* **You learned to use a hundred chart to find numbers before, after, and between other numbers. How is a hundred chart like an organized list?** *(Sample response: Both help us see patterns.)*

Connect to Prior Knowledge of Math ➤ **Sometimes you know more than just the problem. Sometimes you have clues to the answer. What does a clue tell you?** *(Sample responses: A clue tells us what could be a right answer. A clue tells us what could be a wrong answer.)*

Draw a 3 × 3 portion of a hundred chart as shown below. The first row should show 54, 55, and a blank square. The second row should show 64, a blank square, and 66. The third row should show a blank square, 75, and 76.

Have volunteers come forward to fill in the missing numbers. Ask them what clues they used to find the missing numbers.

54	55	
64		66
	75	76

Dime, Nickel, and Penny

EXTEND LANGUAGE

USE WITH LESSON
3-12

Objective Identify the value of a group of dimes, nickels, and pennies through 99¢.

Materials 40 pencils; 4 rubber bands; *(per pair)* coin models (or coins: 4 pennies, 4 nickels, 4 dimes)

Vocabulary Coin, dime, nickel, penny, cent (¢)

ESL Strategies

Use before **LEARN**

🕐 10 MIN

Focus on Meaning ➤ Tell children that counting by fives and counting by tens can help them count <u>coins</u>. Write "<u>dime</u>," "<u>nickel</u>," and "<u>penny</u>" on the board, showing each coin as you write its name. Ask children to repeat the name of each coin as you display it again. **What coin is this? How many <u>cents</u> is it worth?** As they say the value of each coin, write 10¢, 5¢, and 1¢ on the board.

Let's count the money. Which coin is worth the most? *(The dime)* **How much is 1 dime worth?** *(10¢)* Point to the nickel. **How much is 1 nickel worth?** *(5¢)* Point to the dime and then the nickel, and have children count aloud with you: **10¢, 15¢.** Point to the penny. **How much is 1 penny worth?** *(1¢)* Point to the dime, then the nickel, then the penny, and have children count aloud with you: **10¢, 15¢, 16¢.**

Have Students ➤ Report Back Orally

Divide the class into pairs and give each pair 4 pennies, 4 nickels, and 4 dimes. Have children count the coins, reminding them to start counting with the coins of greatest value. Ask the children in each pair to take turns counting aloud the value of each coin set, and then have each pair report orally the total value of all of the coins in the set. *(64¢)*

Quarter and Half-Dollar

ACCESS CONTENT

Objective Count a collection of coins that includes half-dollars, quarters, dimes, nickels, and pennies.

Materials *(per child)* Coin models or coins: half-dollars, quarters, dimes, nickels, pennies; Hundred Chart (Workmat 6)

Vocabulary Quarter, half-dollar

ESL Strategies **Use before** **LEARN** ⏱ 10 MIN

Use Manipulatives ➤ Pass out pennies, nickels, dimes, and <u>quarters</u> to each child, naming them as you pass them out. Have children repeat the names after you. Hold up a quarter. **What is the name of this coin?** *(Quarter)* **Write "quarter" on the board. How much is a quarter worth?** *(25¢)* Write 25¢ on the board. Do the same with <u>half-dollars</u>.

How can you show 25¢ without using a quarter? Have children use the workmat to model their answers. *(Students can use any combination of pennies, nickels, or dimes that equal 25¢.)*

Use Small-Group ➤ Divide the class into pairs, and have them find combinations of 50¢. Draw
Interactions a chart on the board with the headings 25¢, 10¢, 5¢, and 1¢. Ask volunteers to count aloud the coins in one of their combinations in this order: quarters, dimes, nickels, and then pennies. List on the board the number of each coins that they used under the appropriate heading. Point to the combination. **A half-dollar is the same amount of money as this group of coins. It is worth 50¢.** Ask other volunteers to count aloud their combinations.

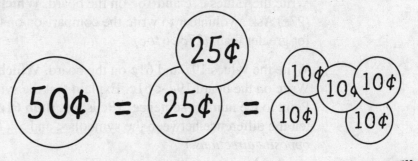

Counting Sets of Coins

ACCESS CONTENT; ACTIVATE PRIOR KNOWLEDGE/BUILD BACKGROUND

Objective Count collections of coins that include half-dollars, quarters, dimes, nickels, and pennies.

Materials *(per child)* Drawing paper; *(per pair)* coin models, or coins: 1 half-dollar, 3 quarters, 5 dimes, 5 nickels, 4 pennies

Use Pictures ➤ Give children drawing paper and ask them to draw a picture of an object. If children get stuck, suggest some types of objects, such as toys, books, food, or clothing. After they complete their drawings, have them write the name of the object above the drawing. Then ask them to give the object a price between 40¢ and 99¢ and to write the price beside the drawing.

Use Role Playing ➤ Divide the class into pairs and have partners exchange drawings. Give each pair 1 half-dollar, 3 quarters, 5 dimes, 5 nickels, and 4 pennies. **Look at the price of the object your partner drew. Use the coins to buy it from him or her.** Ask volunteers to show the picture of the objects they bought and to name its price and what coins they used to pay for it. Have children use this structure: "This is a (name of object). It costs (price of object). I used (names and quantities of coins) to buy it."

Comparing Sets of Coins

USE WITH LESSON **3-15**

ACTIVATE PRIOR KNOWLEDGE/BUILD BACKGROUND; EXTEND LANGUAGE

Objective Compare the values of two sets of coins.

Materials Coin models, or coins: quarters, dimes, nickels, pennies

ESL Strategies

Use before CHECK ✓

🕐 10 MIN

Connect to Prior Knowledge of Math ➤ Write 44¢ and 52¢ on the board. Have a volunteer name the values. **Which is more, 44¢ or 52¢?** *(52¢)* Write on the board 52¢ > 44¢. Review that the symbol > means greater than. Point to the number sentence: **52¢ is greater than 44¢.**

Write the values 27¢ and 16¢ on the board. **Which is greater, 27¢ or 16¢?** *(27¢)* Ask a volunteer to write the comparison on the board using the symbol for greater than. *(27¢ > 16¢)*

Write the values 19¢ and 61¢ on the board. **Which is less, 19¢ or 61¢?** *(19¢)* Write on the board 19¢ < 61¢. Explain that the symbol < means *less than*. Point to the number sentence: **19¢ is less than 61¢.** Ask children how to tell the difference between the symbols < and >. *(The symbols "point" in opposite directions.)*

Have Students Report Back in Writing ➤ Display 2 dimes, 1 nickel, and 1 penny. **Let us count the coins.** Count aloud with children, beginning with the 2 dimes: **10¢, 20¢, 25¢, 26¢.** Write 26¢ on the board. Display 4 dimes and 4 pennies. **How much are these coins?** *(10¢, 20¢, 30¢, 40¢, 41¢, 42¢, 43¢, 44¢)* Have a volunteer lead the class in counting the coins aloud. Write 44¢ on the board. **Which is greater, 26¢ or 44¢?** *(44¢)* **Write this as a number sentence using one of the symbols you just learned.** *(44¢ > 26¢)* Continue with other values that will require children to use both < and >.

Ways to Show the Same Amount

USE WITH LESSON 3-16

ACCESS CONTENT; EXTEND LANGUAGE

Objective Show the same amount of money using different sets of coins.

Materials Small box; coins: half-dollars, quarters, dimes, nickels, pennies

Vocabulary Tally marks, record

ESL Strategies

Use before CHECK ✓

🕐 15 MIN

Use Real Objects ➤ Divide the class into pairs. On the board, write "half-dollars," "quarters," "dimes," "nickels," "pennies," and "total." Have one partner copy the list onto a piece of paper.

Tell children that they are going to play a guessing game. Hold up a small box with some coins in it. **You will try to guess how many cents I have in here.** Tell children that they will be able to ask you only questions using this pattern: "How many (name of coin) do you have?" In turn, you will tell them how many of that coin you have in the box. Tell the pairs to use <u>tally marks</u> next to the coin's name to <u>record</u> the number of each coin in the box. Demonstrate how to use tally marks to be sure all children know what they are.

Have Students Report Back Orally ➤ After you have answered questions about how many half-dollars, quarters, dimes, nickels, and pennies are in the box, pairs should work out how many cents are in the box. Have a volunteer tell you both the total number of cents and how many of each coin are in the box. If the child answers correctly, ask the child's partner to write the total cents on the board. Then ask all pairs what other combinations of coins could make that same amount. Children can either report their answers orally or show by tally marks on a coin model.

Making Change

USE WITH LESSON 3-17

ACTIVATE PRIOR KNOWLEDGE/BUILD BACKGROUND

Objective Count on from the price of an object up to the greater amount paid in order to make change.

Materials Classroom items, such as a board eraser; coins: half-dollars, quarters, dimes, nickels, pennies

Vocabulary Change, price

ESL Strategies

Use before LEARN

🕐 10–15 MIN

Connect to Prior Experiences ➤ Discuss with children experiences they have had buying things at stores. **Have you ever used money to buy something?** Focus the discussion on times when children did not have the exact amount of money for their purchases. **What happens when you give the person in the store more money than what something costs?** *(He or she gives you some money back.)* Explain to children that the money they get back is called <u>change</u>.

Tell the class that you're going to play "Store" and ask two children to volunteer. Give the "customer" 4 dimes and the "storekeeper" an eraser with a tag that reads "38¢." Instruct the customer to enter the store and to ask the storekeeper, "What is the <u>price</u> of the eraser?" The storekeeper refers to the price on the board and says, "This eraser costs 38¢." Ask the class: **If the customer gives the storekeeper 40¢, will he or she get change back?** *(Yes)* **Why?** *(40¢ is more than 38¢.)* Explain to children that they can count on to make change. **Start with the price of the eraser: 38¢. Then count on to the amount paid.** Display a penny as you count on by ones: **39¢, 40¢. I counted on by 2 to get 40¢. That means the customer will get back 2¢ in change.** Repeat the process with other items.

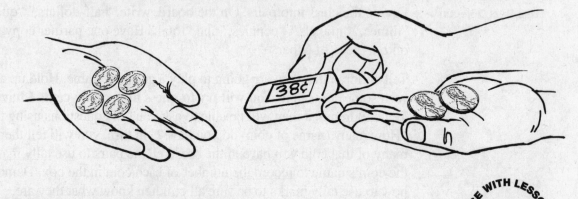

Dollar Bill and Dollar Coin

ACCESS CONTENT

USE WITH LESSON
3-18

Objective Identify the value of a dollar bill and a dollar coin.

Materials Coin model; bill model; 2 $1 bills; assorted coins in sets totaling either $1.00 or 50¢

Vocabulary Dollar sign, dollar bill, decimal point

ESL Strategies *Use before* **LEARN** 🕐 10 MIN

Use Manipulatives ➤ To introduce the dollar, display a <u>dollar bill</u>. Then form several sets of coins that equal a dollar. Include such sets as 100 pennies; 4 quarters; 10 dimes; 20 nickels; 2 quarters plus 5 dimes; 5 dimes plus 1 half-dollar; and 10 nickels plus 2 quarters. Have children count aloud with you as you count each set starting with the coin(s) of greatest value to the coin(s) of least value. Show that the value of each set is 100¢.

Use Demonstration ➤ **What is 100¢ called?** *(A dollar)* **The value of a dollar is 100¢, the same as the value of each set of coins we just counted.** Write $1.00 on the board. Point to the <u>dollar sign</u>. **This sign is called a dollar sign.** Then point to the <u>decimal point</u>. **This point separates the dollars from the cents. It is called a decimal point.** Gesture to the dollar amount, then to the cents amount, indicating that the dollars are written before the decimal point and that the cents are written after it. Write $3.61 on the board. **How many dollars are in this amount?** *(3 dollars)* **How many cents?** *(61 cents)* Repeat with other dollar and cent amounts.

Display 1 quarter, 7 dimes, and 5 pennies. **Do these coins have the same value as a half-dollar or a dollar?** *(A dollar)* Repeat with other sets of coins totaling either 50¢ or $1.

Problem-Solving Applications: Money, Money, Money

EXTEND LANGUAGE

Objective Review and apply key concepts, skills, and strategies learned in this and previous chapters.

ESL Strategies   ***Use after*** **LEARN**   🕐 15 MIN

Have Students
Create Test Items ➤ Divide the class into pairs. Have pairs read to each other the *Writing in Math* story that they wrote in their Journal about money. Then have them write any money comparison number problems that they found in each others' stories in their Journal.

Ask a volunteer to come forward and write the number sentence for a comparison problem that he or she found on the board. Have children identify the way they would solve those problems, based on what they have learned in this chapter about making an organized list, finding the closest ten, counting and comparing sets of coins, or any other method.

Adding Tens

USE WITH LESSON **4-1**

EXTEND LANGUAGE; ACTIVATE PRIOR KNOWLEDGE/BUILD BACKGROUND

Objective Add a multiple of 10 to a two-digit number using models or mental math.

Vocabulary Mental math

ESL Strategies

Use before **LEARN**

⏱ 10 MIN

Focus on Meaning ➤ Write "<u>mental math</u>" on the board. **There are different ways to do math. You can use models or objects. You can also use paper and pencil. How can you do math without using anything?** *(You can do math in your head.)* **Ask children a simple math question, such as "What is 1 plus 1?"** *(2)* **You just did** *mental math*. **When you do mental math, you think the answer through in your mind, or head.**

Connect to Prior ➤ Suggest other simple problems to illustrate mental math. **How much is 5 + 5?**
Knowledge of *(10)* **How did you find the answer?** *(I figured it out in my head.)* **How much**
Math **is 8 + 7?** *(15)* **7 + 3 + 9?** *(19)* **How did you find the answers?** *(Sample answers: I used doubles plus 1; I broke 3 + 9 into 2 + 10 to make it easier to add in my head.)* **Try adding 12 to 20.** Group children into pairs. Have one child model or use paper and pencil; have the other child use mental math to find the answer. Have each child explain their work to the other.

Adding Ones

USE WITH LESSON **4-2**

ACTIVATE PRIOR KNOWLEDGE/BUILD BACKGROUND

Objective Add a one-digit number to a two-digit number using models or mental math.

Materials Workmat 3

ESL Strategies

Use before **LEARN**

⏱ 5–10 MIN

Connect to Prior ➤ **You know how to make 10 to add. When you add ones to a two-digit**
Knowledge of **number, sometimes you have enough ones altogether to make another ten.**
Math

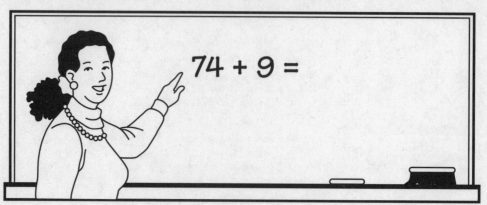

Write 74 + 9 = ___ on the board. **Let's use mental math to break apart the number 9. How should you break it apart if you add it to 74?** *(Break it into 6 + 3.)* **Now let's add 74 to 6 and 3.** Under the first number sentence, write 74 + 6 + 3 = ___. Ask a volunteer to explain what the next step should be. *(Add 74 + 6.)* **What is the sum of 74 and 6?** *(80)* **What should we do next?** *(Add 3 to 80.)* **What is the final sum?** *(83)* Read the completed number sentence aloud with children: **74 plus 6 plus 3 equals 83.**

Write other number sentences, such as 35 + 7 = ___, on the board, and repeat the process.

Adding Tens and Ones

USE WITH LESSON 4-3

ACCESS CONTENT; EXTEND LANGUAGE

Objective Add a two-digit number to a two-digit number using models or mental math.

Materials *(per group)* Connecting cubes

ESL Strategies

Use before CHECK ✓

⏱ 10 MIN

Use Manipulatives ➤ Divide the class into groups of four that are each made up of 2 pairs. Distribute enough cubes for each pair to do two-digit addition. Write 32 + 16 = ___ on the board. Have one pair in the group use cubes to add the tens and then add the ones. Have the other pair use mental math to get the sum. Ask each pair to tell the other how they added to get the sum. **One pair used a model. The other pair used mental math. Are the sums the same?** Have children in the group check to make sure their sums are the same. If not, review the steps of each process.

Have Students Report Back Orally ➤ Write other, similar number sentences (without using regrouping) on the board. Have pairs in each group alternate using mental math and cubes to find the sum. Have them check to make sure they got the same sums. Then have pairs in the group explain to each other how they got their results.

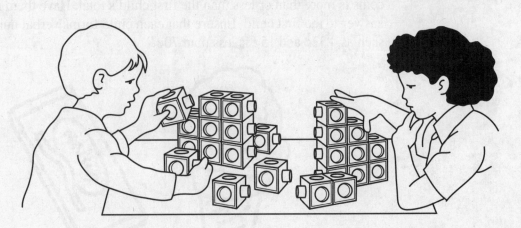

Estimating Sums

ACCESS CONTENT; EXTEND LANGUAGE

Objective Estimate the sum of 2 two-digit numbers.

Materials *(per group)* Coins totaling about $2

Vocabulary Estimate

ESL Strategies **Use before** LEARN

⏱ 10–15 MIN

Focus on Meaning ➤ **<u>Estimate</u> means to "find out about how much." When you estimate the answer to a problem, you do not find an exact answer. You estimate to find an answer that is close to an exact answer.** *Estimate* **can also mean the result you get when you figure out a problem.** Point out to the children the two pronunciations of *estimate*. **An** *estimate* **is not an exact answer. What are some ways you have learned to find an exact answer?** *(Doubles facts, making 10, related facts)* **Let's think of a time when you don't need an exact answer.** Write 50¢ on the board. **If you go to a toy store with 50¢ and want two 19¢ toys, do you have enough money?** *(Yes)* **We can find out by estimating.** Write 19¢ twice on the board. **What is the nearest ten to 19?** *(20)* Cross out 19¢ in both places and write 20¢. **What is 20 + 20?** *(40)* **Is 50 more than the sum of two 20s?** *(Yes)* **You estimated to figure out if you had enough money.**

Now write 39¢ on the board. **What if you want two 39¢ toys? Do you have enough money?** *(No)* **What is the nearest ten to 39?** *(40)* Cross out 39¢ and write 40¢. **Is 40 + 40 bigger or smaller than 50?** *(Bigger)* **When can you estimate?** *(If you want to know if a sum is big enough/small enough.)*

Use Manipulatives ➤ Put children into groups of three. Distribute coins. Have one child in each group pick out coins, adding to a multiple of 10 cents. Have the other two children pick several coins at random, count the coins, and tell each other how much they have. Then have the two children estimate whether the sum of their coins is more than or less than the first child's total. Have them report their answer to the first child. Ensure that each child forms verbal number sentences such as, "32¢ and 15¢ is less than 70¢."

Subtracting Tens

ACTIVATE PRIOR KNOWLEDGE/BUILD BACKGROUND; EXTEND LANGUAGE

Objective Subtract a multiple of 10 from a two-digit number using models or mental math.

ESL Strategies   *Use before* **LEARN**   ⏵ 10 MIN

Connect to Prior Knowledge of Math ➤ On the board write, "3 tens + 5 tens = ____." **What is another way to write this addition problem?** *(30 + 50)* **What addition fact can you use to add the tens?** *(3 + 5 = 8)* Explain that 3 tens plus 5 tens equals 8 tens. **What is another way to write 8 tens?** *(80)* **You know how to add tens. Now we are going to subtract tens.**

Write "5 tens − 3 tens = ____" on the board. Point to the minus sign and the equal sign as you read the problem aloud with children. **This is a subtraction problem. You are going to find the difference between the two numbers. Can you think of another way to write this problem?** *(50 − 30)* Underneath the subtraction problem write 50 − 30 = ____. Read the problem aloud with the children. Then display 5 tens models. **How many tens should I take away to find the difference?** *(3)* **How many tens are left?** *(2)* Write "2 tens" on the first blank after the equals sign. Point to 50 − 30 = ____ **What number should I write after the equals sign here?** *(20)*

Have Students Report Back in Writing ➤ Have children work in pairs using paper and pencil. **I'm going to say a subtraction problem, such as 4 tens minus 1 ten.** Have children work with their partner to write out the problem using numbers, such as 40 − 10 = ____. Then have the pairs find the difference. **After you find the difference, both partners should raise their hands, and I will check your answers. Let's try a practice problem. 3 tens minus 2 tens equals what?** *(30 − 20 = 10)* Once children understand the instructions, give them subtraction problems, such as "5 tens minus 1 ten," "7 tens minus 2 tens," and "9 tens minus 6 tens."

Subtracting Tens and Ones

ACCESS CONTENT; EXTEND LANGUAGE

Objective Subtract a two-digit number from a two-digit number using models or mental math.

Materials Number cards from 10–17; *(per pair)* connecting cubes

ESL Strategies   *Use before* **CHECK** ✓   ⏱ 10–15 MIN

Use Manipulatives ➤ Divide the class into pairs. Assign each pair a two-digit number greater than 20, with either 8 or 9 in the ones place. Have one child in each pair use connecting cubes to model the pair's number. **I am going to hold up a number card. Subtract my number from your number.** Have one partner subtract by taking away cubes. Then have the other partner write a subtraction sentence. Have the partners switch roles each time you hold up a new card. Repeat a few times, so that each partner has a couple of chances to perform each role.

Have Students ➤ Have a volunteer come forward to write one of the subtraction sentences on
Report Back   the board. Lead children in reading the sentences aloud. Repeat a few times
in Writing   so that several children have a chance to report back.

Estimating Differences

USE WITH LESSON
4-7

EXTEND LANGUAGE; ACCESS CONTENT

Objective Determine whether the difference between a multiple of 10 and another amount is more or less than a given multiple of 10.

Vocabulary More, less

ESL Strategies   ***Use before*** **LEARN**   🕐 10–15 MIN

Focus on Meaning ➤ **You know how to compare two numbers. <u>More</u> means "greater than."** Write > on the board. **This symbol, or sign, shows that the number before the symbol is greater than the number after it. If one number is greater than another number, it is *more* than that number. What are some other math words that have the same meaning as *greater than*?** (*Higher number, bigger number, larger number*)

You know the word <u>less</u>. Write < on the board. **This symbol means "less than." The number before the symbol is less than the number after the symbol. What are some other math words that have the same meaning as *less*?** (*Lower number, smaller number, fewer*)

Use Pictures ➤ **Draw two groups of pictures on a page. You can draw anything you like—dogs, flowers, balls, hats.** Make sure children understand that they should draw a different number of items in one group than in the other. **Circle the group that has more. Write the word *less* next to the other group.** (*Drawings will vary.*)

Problem-Solving Strategy:
Try, Check, and Revise

USE WITH LESSON
4-8

EXTEND LANGUAGE; ACCESS CONTENT

Objective Solve a problem by finding pairs of numbers, the sums of which are a given multiple of 10.

Materials Student journals

Vocabulary Revise

Use before **LEARN**

⏱ 10–15 MIN

Have Students ➤
Report Back
Orally

When you <u>revise</u> something, you look to see if you should change it.
Sometimes when you want to solve a problem, you try an answer.
If the answer doesn't work, you see what you have learned. You
look at it again, and you change it. You revise it. Revise starts with
re-. Many words in English start with *re-*. **Can you think of some
of them? Write some down in your journal.** Split the class into small
groups of three or four. Have partners share *re-* words, and help each
other define them. Have volunteers tell you their group's *re-* words
and give a short-form answer or short sentence telling what the words
mean. After a few examples, ask children what is the same about the
words.

Use ➤
Demonstration

Write "7 + ___ = 10" on the board. **I'm going to find a number to add to
7 that sums to 10. I'll try 4.** Write 4 in the blank. **Let's check. Is that
right?** *(No, 7 + 4 = 11)* **OK, let's revise my try. Should I try a larger
number or a smaller number?** *(Smaller)* **How do you know?** *(11 is larger
than 10)* **What should I try?** *(3)* Erase the 4 and replace it with 3. **Let's
check. Is that right?** *(Yes, 7 + 3 = 10)*

Addition and Subtraction Patterns

USE WITH LESSON
4-9

EXTEND LANGUAGE

Objective Discover a numeric pattern made by repeatedly adding or subtracting
the same number.

Materials 5 sets of 3 classroom objects, such as an eraser, a pencil, and a pad
of paper

Vocabulary Pattern

Use before **LEARN**

⏱ 15 MIN

Focus on Meaning ➤

Arrange 3 different types of classroom objects, such as an eraser, a pencil,
and a pad of paper, in a <u>pattern</u> that repeats at least twice. Point to the items.
**Eraser, pencil, pad of paper; eraser, pencil, pad of paper. What comes
next?** *(Eraser)* **This is a pattern. In a pattern, you can tell what comes
next by what has come before. In this case, the same order happens
again and again.** Have a volunteer come forward and continue the pattern,
naming the objects as he or she places them in the pattern.

Have Students ➤
Report Back
Orally

Group the class into pairs. Have each child use objects in the room to make a
pattern for his or her partner to continue. Have pairs describe their patterns
verbally to each other.

You can make patterns with numbers, too. Write 11, 21, 31, and 41 on the
board. Read the numbers with the class. **Which number comes next?** *(51)*
What is the pattern? *(Add 10 to each number.)* **You add ten each time.**
Write these two number patterns on the board: 10, 8, 6, 4; 18, 15, 12, 9.
What pattern do you see in each group of numbers? *(The numbers get
smaller by 2 in the first pattern; the numbers get smaller by 3 in the second*

pattern.) Have each pair create a number pattern. Have a child from each group show their pattern to the class and explain the pattern.

Finding Parts of 100

USE WITH LESSON 4-10

ACTIVATE PRIOR KNOWLEDGE/BUILD BACKGROUND; ACCESS CONTENT

Objective Find the missing part of 100 when the given part is a multiple of 5 or 10.

Materials *(per pair)* Coins

ESL Strategies   *Use before* **LEARN**   🕐 10 MIN

Connect to Prior Knowledge of Math ➤ Display four quarters next to a dollar bill, and three quarters, two dimes and a nickel next to another dollar bill. **You know that a dollar is 100¢.** Point to the first set of coins. **One quarter is 25¢. How many cents are in four quarters?** (100¢) Point to the dollar bill. **This is a dollar. It's 100¢, too.** Have a volunteer come forward. **I'm going to take away a coin and give it to you.** Hand the child a quarter. **How many cents are left?** *(75¢)* **How many cents do you have?** *(25¢)* Write 75¢ + 25¢ = 100¢ on the board. Take the quarter back. Now point to the second set of coins, and again take away a coin—this time a dime. Go through the same process with the child, and write the addition sentence 90¢ + 10¢ = 100¢ on the board.

Use Manipulatives ➤ Group the children into pairs, and give each pair paper and pencil, two quarters, and fifty cents made up of other coins. Have one partner take away one or two coins. Have the other partner write the corresponding addition sentence, then read it aloud. Then have the partners switch roles.

Ask for volunteers to come forward and write one of their addition sentences on the board. Have the volunteers read the sentences to the class.

Problem-Solving Skill: Look Back and Check

USE WITH LESSON 4-11

EXTEND LANGUAGE

Objective "Look back and check" is a strategy that can help confirm the solution to a problem.

Use before LEARN ◔ 15 MIN

Focus on Meaning ➤ **How can you tell if an answer makes sense? You can sometimes find clue words in a problem that let you know.** Write these word problems on the board:

> Anna has 8 new kittens. She gives away 5 to friends. How many kittens does she have left?

> Luis has 22 CDs. His father gives him 4 more for his birthday. How many CDs does Luis have now?

Point to the first problem. **How can you write a number sentence for this problem?** *(8 − 5 = 3)* **Let's look at the problem to check whether the number sentence is right. How did you tell whether to add or subtract? What clues tell you to add or subtract?** *(The problem says she gives away kittens; the problem asks how many kittens she has left.)*

Point to the second problem. **How can you write a number sentence for this problem?** Repeat the process above, this time with addition.

Have Students ➤ Divide the class into pairs. Ask one partner to write a math story with a
Report Back   problem. Have the other partner write the number sentence to solve the
in Writing   problem. Have the first child check the answer by circling the clue words in
                 the story. Then have the pair tell how they know whether to add or subtract.

Problem-Solving Applications:
Take Me Out to the Ballgame!

USE WITH LESSON

4-12

EXTEND LANGUAGE

Objective Review and apply key concepts, skills, and strategies learned in this and previous chapters.

Use after LEARN ◔ 15 MIN

Have Students ➤ Divide the class into large groups (four or more). Ask each group to work
Report Back   together to write a short story about baseball, soccer, or another team sport
Orally   they know about. Tell children they can write about a game that they played

or watched, or they can write about a game they make up. Tell them to make sure to include how many points were scored and other number details. If there are some groups that would prefer not to write about sports, allow them to write a story about another topic with number details.

Have one child from each group volunteer to read the group's story aloud. Have the volunteer make up one or two number sentences based on the story and write them on the board. Then have the class decide if they can find more than one way to solve each number sentence. Remind them to consider estimation, adding tens and ones, subtracting tens and ones, or any other lesson from this chapter.

Adding With and Without Regrouping
ACCESS CONTENT

Objective Regroup 10 ones as 1 ten when adding.

Materials *(per group)* Connecting cubes; labeled white index cards; labeled colored index cards; two-foot piece of yarn; paper; pencil

Vocabulary Regroup, sum

ESL Strategies **Use before** CHECK ✓   ⏱ 15 MIN

Use Manipulatives ➤ Organize children into five groups. On the white index cards, write the numbers 16, 18, 27, 29, and 36 (one number per card). On the colored index cards, write the numbers 4, 5, 6, 7, and 8 (one number per card). Give each group one white index card, one colored index card, connecting cubes, and yarn. Ask one member of each group to look at the white card and count out that many tens and ones. Ask another member of each group to look at the colored card and count out that many ones. **What is the <u>sum</u> of the ones from both cards?** *(Answers will vary.)* **Do you have enough ones to <u>regroup</u> 10 ones for 1 ten?** *(Yes)* Have students place the yarn around the cubes they will regroup. Have the group check by counting the encircled ones aloud. Remind children that the ring of yarn should enclose exactly 10 ones cubes.

Ask a group member to trade the ones for a ten. Then ask each group to report the numbers on the index cards, the sum of those numbers, and the sum of all their cubes since regrouping. Note to students that the sum is the same before and after regrouping.

Recording Addition
ACCESS CONTENT; EXTEND LANGUAGE

Objective Add a one-digit number to a two-digit number, regroup, and record the process in the vertical format.

Materials *(per child)* Connecting cubes; Place-Value Mat A (Workmat 4); two-foot piece of yarn

ESL Strategies **Use before** LEARN   ⏱ 15 MIN

Use Gestures ➤ Write 36 + 9 vertically on the board. **We are going to add a two-digit and a one-digit number.** Distribute connecting cubes, Workmats, and pieces of yarn. Ask children to display 36 and 9 on their Workmats. Write "Tens" and "Ones" above the appropriate columns of digits on the board. Ask a child to add 6 ones + 9 ones. *(15 ones)* Then ask the class whether the child needs to regroup. **Show a "thumbs up" if you think we need to regroup. Show a "thumbs down" if you think that we do not need to regroup. Why?** *(Children should* *display a thumbs up. We cannot put more than 9 ones in the ones column.)* **How should we write the sum, 15 ones?** *(Write the 5 ones below the line in the ones column. Draw a box at the top of the tens column. Write a 1 in that box.)* Check to be sure children make a ring of yarn around 10 ones and then exchange those 10 ones for a ten. **How do we add the numbers in the tens column?** *(1 ten + 3 tens = 4 tens = 40)* Write the answer. **What is the sum of 36 + 9?** *(45)*

Have Students ➤
Report Back
in Writing

Write 45 + 3 vertically on the board. Ask children to solve the problem using connecting cubes. Then ask the children whether they need to regroup and to explain why or why not. *(No. The sum of the ones in the ones column is less than 10.)* Ask a volunteer to come forward and show how to record the sum. Repeat the process several more times with several other two-digit plus one-digit sums, most of which should need regrouping. For each problem, have children find the sum using place-value models, then ask a child to come forward to record the sum on the board.

Adding Two-Digit Numbers
With and Without Regrouping

USE WITH LESSON
5-3

ACCESS CONTENT

Objective Use the standard algorithm to add 2 two-digit numbers with and without regrouping.

Materials Pens; desks; chairs (more than 10 of each positioned in easy-to-spot places around the room)

Vocabulary Two-digit numbers

ESL Strategies **Use before** LEARN

🕐 10–15 MIN

Use Real Objects ➤ Write the words "pencil," "pen," "desk," and "chair" on the board. Be sure that there are enough of each item to be counted into double digits. Have children say the words aloud with you. Then place children into four groups. Assign each group one of the objects written on the board and ask group members to search the classroom and count all those objects that are visible in the room. (Tell children that they are not allowed to open any desks, drawers, or bags during their search.)

When the groups finish counting the objects, ask each group in turn, **How many (name of object) are there in the room?** Ask the group to answer in a complete sentence. Then have a volunteer from each group come forward and write the total number on the board under the appropriate word. Point to the word *pencil* on the board and its corresponding number. **How many pencils are in the room?** Continue for the other three objects.

All four of these numbers are <u>two-digit numbers</u>. We are going to learn how to add two-digit numbers. Let's find out how many pencils and pens are in the classroom. Write the total number of pens under the total number of pencils to form a vertical addition problem. Beside each number draw the appropriate number of tens and ones models. Point to the ones column on the board. **Do we need to regroup?** *(Answer will depend on the numbers in the addition problem.)* Help children complete the addition problem. **What is the sum? How many pencils and pens are there in the classroom?** *(Answers will vary.)* Repeat the procedure for two other combinations of objects.

Practice with Two-Digit Addition

ACCESS CONTENT; EXTEND LANGUAGE

USE WITH LESSON
5-4

Objective Use the standard algorithm symbolically to add two-digit numbers with and without regrouping.

Materials Tens models and ones models; Place-Value Mat A (Workmat 4)

ESL Strategies | **Use before** **LEARN**   🕐 10–15 MIN

Use Manipulatives ➤ Display 4 tens and 5 ones models on a Workmat. Ask children how many tens models and ones models they see. *(4 tens and 5 ones)* **What number do the models show?** *(45)* Add 16 more ones models. **I have 4 tens and 5 ones plus 16 more ones. Do I have enough ones to regroup?** *(Yes; 5 + 6 is more than 10.)* Direct a child to place a piece of yarn around 10 of the 11 ones models, forming a ring. Have another child count the ones models inside the ring aloud and regroup them into a ten. **How many tens models and ones models are there now?** *(6 tens and 1 one)* **What number do they show?** *(61)* **What is the sum of 45 and 16?** *(61)* **Did we have to regroup to find this sum?** *(Yes)* Write 45 + 16 = 61 in vertical form on the board.

Have Students ➤ Write another two-digit addition problem, such as 64 + 37 = ____ on the
Report Back   board. Ask a child volunteer to come forward and model the problem on the
in Writing   workmat for the class. Guide the child through the steps of the addition process, having the child record the solution on the board. Repeat the process with several children.

Adding Money

ACTIVATE PRIOR KNOWLEDGE/BUILD BACKGROUND; ACCESS CONTENT

USE WITH LESSON
5-5

Objective Add two money amounts (less than $1.00) using paper and pencil.

Use before LEARN ⏱ 10 MIN

Connect to Prior ➤ Write on the board: "Julio had 63¢. Then his uncle gave him a quarter.
Knowledge of How much money does he have now?" Read the sentences aloud and then
Math read them together with children. **How much money did Jerry have at
first?** *(63¢)* **How much money did he receive?** *(A quarter, 25¢)* **How can
you find out how much money he has now?** *(Add 63¢ and 25¢.)* Write
63¢ + 25¢ on the board and ask a volunteer to come forward and find the
sum. **How much money does Julio have in all?** *(He has 88¢.)* Encourage
complete sentence responses by modeling.

Expand Student ➤ Write on the board: "Lucia has 57¢. She finds 35¢ in her coat pocket. How
Responses much money does she have now?" Again read the sentences aloud, then read
them with children. Ask a volunteer to come forward and write the responses on
the board as a vertical addition problem. **How much money did Lucia have at
first?** *(57¢)* **How much money did she find?** *(35¢)* **How can you find out
how much money she has now?** *(Add 57¢ and 35¢.)* **How much money does
Lucia have in all?** *(She has 92¢.)* Again, encourage complete sentence
responses by modeling. Repeat the procedure using other amounts.

Adding Three Numbers

USE WITH LESSON
5-6

ACCESS CONTENT

Objective Add 3 two-digit numbers with paper and pencil.

Materials Number Cards 0–11 (Teaching Tool 7); Number Cards 12–20
(Teaching Tool 9); *(per group)* paper bag; index cards numbered from 11–40

Use before CHECK ✓ ⏱ 10–15 MIN

Use ➤ Place index cards numbered between 11 and 40 in a paper bag. Ask two
Demonstration volunteers to come forward. Have the first pick a card from the bag, read the
number aloud, and write the number on the board. Have the second pick an
index card from the bag, read the number aloud, and write the number on the
board as a vertical addition problem. **Now I will show you a number card
and write the number as the third addend, or third number to add. Use
fact strategies to add the numbers.** Show a number card, and guide
children through the solution if needed.

Use Small-Group ➤ Divide the class into a few
Interactions groups. Give each group a paper
bag and a set of numbered index
cards. Instruct them to follow
the procedure as demonstrated
to select two numbers, then to
wait for you to display a number
card. Have the groups solve their
resulting addition problem,
using fact strategies if possible.

Problem-Solving Skill: Use Data from a Table

ACCESS CONTENT

Objective Solve problems involving addition by using data from a table.

Vocabulary Table, data

ESL Strategies | **Use before** LEARN | ⏱ 10 MIN

Use Real Objects ➤ Draw a <u>table</u> on the board with three columns and two rows. In the top row, write one of these headings in each box: "White Shirt," "Colored Shirt," "Striped Shirt." **Raise your hand if you are wearing a white shirt.** Count the raised hands and write the number on the board under the White Shirt heading. Repeat this to fill in the Colored Shirt and Striped Shirt columns. Point to the board and tell children that they have made a table.

Use Graphic ➤ **A table is a way to show facts or information. We call the facts in a table**
Organizers **the** <u>data</u>**. Look at the table. How many children are wearing white shirts?** *(Answers will vary.)* Ask the same question for the other two columns. **How can we use the table to find how many children have colored shirts and striped shirts?** *(By adding together the number in the "Colored Shirt" column and the "Striped Shirt" column)* Accept short-form answers and gestures if children are not ready to produce a complete sentence. Write the two numbers on the board and make an addition problem. Ask a volunteer to solve the problem. **We can also use the table to compare two pieces of data. Are there more striped shirts or colored shirts in the classroom?** *(Answers will vary.)* **What is the total number of those kinds of shirts?** Ask a volunteer to solve the problem.

Estimating Sums

ACTIVATE PRIOR KNOWLEDGE/BUILD BACKGROUND

Objective Estimate a sum as a multiple of 10 and compare the estimate to the exact sum.

Materials *(per group)* Coin Models (Teaching Tool 14); 4 sticky notes; eraser; book; set of pencils; pad of paper

Vocabulary Estimate

ESL Strategies | **Use before** LEARN | ⏱ 5–10 MIN

Use Simulation ➤ Display classroom objects with price tags made from sticky notes. For example, tag the chalkboard eraser with a price of 27¢, the book with a price of 46¢, the set of pencils with a price of 14¢, and the pad of paper with a price of 22¢.

You already know how to <u>estimate</u> **sums. First you add the tens. Next you add the ones, and see if that makes another 10. Then you can find out whether the sum you estimate is greater than or less than the exact sum.**

Organize children into several groups, and distribute coin models totaling 89¢ to each group. Ask a child in each group to count the coin models and tell their group how much money they have. Ask another child in each group to estimate whether the group can buy a combination of the classroom objects that you specify. Vary the set of objects for each group. Have each group report back the objects they are trying to buy and whether they estimate they can buy them. Each group should show how they added the tens and ones, and made their estimate.

**Use ➤
Brainstorming**

Ask the group that estimated the cost of the eraser and the book to tell the class their estimate again. **It helps to know how close your estimate is to the exact answer. What have you learned that can help you do that?** *(Answers will vary: finding the closest 10, look back and check, subtracting two-digit numbers, and others should be suggested.)* Use each of these methods to check the estimated cost of the eraser and book.

Ways to Add

USE WITH LESSON 5-9

ACTIVATE PRIOR KNOWLEDGE/BUILD BACKGROUND; ACCESS CONTENT

Objective Recognize and use different ways to add two-digit numbers.

Materials *(per pair)* Tens and ones models; paper and pencil; Hundred Chart (Workmat 6); calculator

ESL Strategies

Use before LEARN ⏱ 10 MIN

**Connect to Prior
Knowledge of
Language ➤**

Write on the board the terms "cubes," "mental math," "paper and pencil," and "calculator." Pointing to each term, remind children that these are four different ways to add numbers. Write the addition problem 43 + 19 on the board. Point to the word "cubes." **How can you use cubes to add 43 and 19?** Encourage children to answer verbally or by showing the addition with ones models and tens models. Accept all forms of responses, including showing how to find the solution using cubes. Repeat the procedure for the other three terms.

**Use Small-Group
Interactions ➤**

Write six addition problems on the board, such as 23 + 64 and 9 + 37. Group children into pairs. **Pick two of these problems and solve them. For each problem, choose one of the four ways that work best: cubes, mental math, paper and pencil, and calculator.** Give each pair 18 tens models, 18 ones models, paper and pencils, and a calculator. Allow time for each pair to work through their problems. Engage students in a discussion when they have finished. **What is one of the problems you solved? How did you solve it? Why do you think this is the best way to solve the problem?** *(Accept all reasonable responses.)* If children are having trouble describing their addition strategy, ask questions with key words to help them articulate their response.

Problem-Solving Strategy:
Try, Check, and Revise

ACTIVATE PRIOR KNOWLEDGE/BUILD BACKGROUND; ACCESS CONTENT

Objective Solve a problem by estimating, checking the estimate, and then revising the estimate until the final answer is reached.

Materials Number Cards 0–11 (Teaching Tool 7); Number Cards 12–20 (Teaching Tool 9)

ESL Strategies

Use before LEARN

🕐 10–15 MIN

Connect to Prior Knowledge of Math ➤ Divide children into groups of three or four. Display five number cards: 11, 14, 16, 18, and 19. **Use three of these numbers to add up to 51. How can you start?** *(I can estimate. I can use try, check, and revise.)*

Use Peer Questioning ➤ Ask each group to work together to try to find the numbers that add up to 51. For those groups that start slowly, remind them that they can find the nearest ten and estimate, or that they can try to find numbers with ones that add up to a number ending in 1. Monitor children's progress, asking questions such as: **Is the sum of those numbers more than 51?** or **Does the sum of those numbers end in 1?**

After the groups have found the answer *(14 + 18 + 19 = 51)*, display five other number cards, such as 4, 13, 15, 17, and 20, asking groups to find which three of those numbers add up to 37. For this problem, have one child in each group write down the group's number combinations. Select a group or two to report to the class on how they found the answer *(4 + 13 + 20 = 37)*.

Problem-Solving Applications:
The World of Plants

EXTEND LANGUAGE

Objective Review and apply key concepts, skills, and strategies learned in this and previous chapters.

ESL Strategies

Use after LEARN

🕐 15 MIN

Have Students Create Test Items ➤ Have children get together in pairs. Ask them to read to each other the Writing in Math subtraction story they wrote in their journals. Now have them write any two-digit addition problem number sentences they have found in each others' stories in their journals.

Ask two volunteers to come forward and write the additional problems they have found, on the board. Ask children to identify from those problems the way they would find the sum and check their answers, based on the methods they have learned in this chapter

Subtracting With and Without Regrouping

USE WITH LESSON **6-1**

ACTIVATE PRIOR KNOWLEDGE/BUILD BACKGROUND; ACCESS CONTENT

Objective Regroup 1 ten as 10 ones when subtracting.

Materials Connecting cubes (tens and ones models)

Vocabulary Subtract, regroup

ESL Strategies ***Use before*** **LEARN** ⏱ 10 MIN

Connect to Prior ➤
Knowledge of
Math

You know how to <u>regroup</u> to add. Let's see how we regroup to <u>subtract</u>. Use connecting cubes to display a tens model. **How many ones are in 1 ten?** *(10)* **There are 10 ones in 1 ten.** Add another tens model, and display 4 ones beside it. **How many tens are there now?** *(2 tens)* **How many ones are there?** *(4 ones)* Write "2 tens and 4 ones" on the board. **There are 2 tens and 4 ones. What number does this show?** *(24)* Underneath the phrase, write "Subtract 8 ones." Read it aloud with children. **We will subtract 8 ones. Are there enough ones?** *(No)* **No, there are only 4 ones and we need to subtract 8. We need to regroup.** Remove one of the tens models and exchange it for 10 ones. As you do so, explain that you are regrouping. **Now how many tens are there?** *(1 ten)* **How many ones are there?** *(14 ones)* **Can we take away 8 ones now?** *(Yes)* Remove 8 ones. **How many ones are left?** *(6 ones)* **How many tens are left?** *(1 ten)* Write the phrase "1 ten and 6 ones" on the board. **There are 1 ten and 6 ones. What number does this show?** *(16)*

Use Gestures ➤
Display 3 tens and 5 ones. **I need to subtract 4 ones. Do I need to regroup?** *(No)* Ask children to give a "thumbs-up" response if you need to regroup and a "thumbs-down" response if you do not need to regroup. **If I need to subtract 9 ones do I need to regroup?** *(Children should give a "thumbs-up" response.)*

Recording Subtraction

USE WITH LESSON **6-2**

ACCESS CONTENT; EXTEND LANGUAGE

Objective Subtract a one-digit number from a two-digit number with or without regrouping using the standard algorithm.

Materials *(all per child)* Connecting cubes; Place-Value Mat A (Workmat 4); 2-ft piece of yarn

Use before CHECK ✓   🕐 15 MIN

Use Gestures ➤ Distribute connecting cubes, workmats, and pieces of yarn. Write 57 − 9 vertically on the board and have children display this on their workmats. Write "Tens" and "Ones" above each column of digits on the board. Ask the class to subtract 9 ones from 7 ones. **Show a "thumbs up" if you think we need to regroup. Show a "thumbs down" if you think we do not need to regroup.** *(Children should give a thumbs-up response.)* Explain that the correct answer is "thumbs up." **Why?** *(You cannot take away 9 ones from 7 ones.)* Have children make a ring of yarn around 1 ten on their mats and regroup the ten into 10 ones. After they have regrouped, have them remove the yarn. **How should you show the regrouping?** *(Cross out the 7 in the ones column. Draw a little box at the top of the ones column. Write "17" in that box. Cross out the 5 in the tens column. Draw a little box at the top of the tens column. Write "4" in that box.)* **How do you subtract the numbers in the ones column?** *(17 ones − 9 ones = 8 ones)* Have a volunteer write the answer on the board. **What is 57 − 9?** *(48)* Have another volunteer complete the answer on the board.

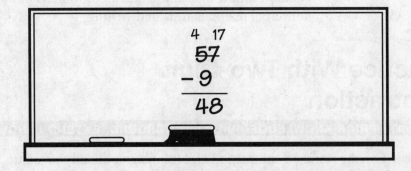

Have Students Report Back in Writing ➤ Write 36 − 4 vertically on the board. Have children use connecting cubes to solve the problem. **Do you need to regroup? Why or why not?** *(No. You can find the difference in the ones column.)* Have a volunteer show how to record the difference on the board. Repeat the process with other examples, most of which should need regrouping. Have children use connecting cubes to solve each problem, and have one child come forward to record the difference on the board.

Subtracting Two-Digit Numbers With or Without Regrouping

USE WITH LESSON
6-3

ACCESS CONTENT

Objective Use the standard subtraction algorithm to subtract a two-digit number from another two-digit number.

Materials *(all per group)* 4 index cards; Number Cards 12–20 (Teaching Tool 9); connecting cubes; Place-Value Mat A (Workmat 4)

Use before CHECK ✓   🕐 10–15 MIN

Use Small-Group ➤
Interactions

Divide the class into groups of four. Give each group connecting cubes and a set of index cards showing the numbers 41, 42, 43, and 44. Have one member from each group choose a card. Have another come forward to choose a number card. Have the third child subtract the smaller number from the larger number, using the connecting cube models and Workmat 4. Have the fourth child record the subtraction problem vertically with the solution. Display the steps for solving subtraction problems:

1. Show the greater number as tens and ones.

2. Regroup 1 ten as 10 ones if needed.

3. Subtract the ones.

4. Subtract the tens.

Repeat the activity four times, so that each child has a chance to perform each step. As they proceed, give guidance to each group, making sure that children follow the subtraction algorithm. Monitor their verbal interaction, nonverbal manipulation, and writing.

Practice With Two-Digit Subtraction

USE WITH LESSON
6-4

ACTIVATE PRIOR KNOWLEDGE/BUILD BACKGROUND; EXTEND LANGUAGE

Objective Use the standard subtraction algorithm symbolically to subtract a two-digit number from another two-digit number.

Materials 65 pennies; Number Cards 12–20 (Teaching Tool 9)

ESL Strategies

Use before CHECK ✓   🕐 10 MIN

Use Role Playing ➤
Have one child play the role of a banker and another child play a bank customer. Give the banker 45 pennies, and have the child organize them into groups of ten. **How many pennies do you have in your bank?** *(45)* **You have 45 pennies in your bank.**

Give the customer one of the number cards as a "check." Have the customer "cash" the check by telling the banker how many pennies the card says to withdraw. Have the customer say, "I would like _____ cents, please."

Focus on Use ➤ After the banker gives the pennies to the customer, address the class. **How many pennies did the banker have?** *(45)* **How many pennies did the customer ask for?** *(Number on the card)* Write the subtraction problem vertically on the board. Have the banker and the customer record the difference on the board.

Repeat the activity with other pairs of students, varying the number of pennies in the bank to provide varied practice.

Problem-Solving Strategy: Write a Number Sentence

USE WITH LESSON
6-5

ACTIVATE PRIOR KNOWLEDGE/BUILD BACKGROUND; EXTEND LANGUAGE

Objective Solve problems by writing number sentences.

Materials 9 pencils

Vocabulary Number sentence

ESL Strategies   *Use before* **LEARN**   ⏱ 5–10 MIN

Connect to Prior Knowledge of Math ➤ **You know that you can write a <u>number sentence</u> to solve a problem.** Display 9 pencils. **How many pencils do I have?** *(9)* Write 9 on the board. **I am going to take 3 pencils away.** Put 3 pencils down. Write − 3 = ___ on the board to form the number sentence 9 − 3 = ___. **How do you finish this number sentence?** *(6)* Count the 6 pencils left to show that the answer makes sense.

Focus on Meaning ➤ **What words told you to subtract to get the right answer?** *(Take away)* **Words in the problem help you understand what to do. What do words like *altogether, in all, sum,* and *total* tell you to do?** *(Add)* **What do words like *more than, left, take away,* and *different* tell you to do?** *(Subtract)* Draw two columns on the board with the headings: "Addition" and "Subtraction." List the clue words for each operation under the appropriate column head. Ask children if they know any other clue words.

Subtracting Money

ACTIVATE PRIOR KNOWLEDGE/BUILD BACKGROUND

Objective Subtract amounts of money less than $1.00 with and without regrouping.

Materials Coin models; connecting cubes; play fruit

Vocabulary Price, change

ESL Strategies

Use before CHECK ✓

🕐 10–15 MIN

Connect to Prior Knowledge of Math ➤ Write on the board: "LeAnne has a quarter. She buys an orange. The <u>price</u> of the orange is 20¢. How much <u>change</u> will LeAnne get back?" Read the problem together with children. **How can you find the answer?** *(Subtract 20¢ from 25¢.)* Write 25¢ − 20¢ on the board. **Taking away 20 cents from 25 cents is the same as taking away 20 cubes from 25 cubes.** Have a volunteer find the difference using the connecting cubes. **How much change does LeAnne get?** *(She gets 5¢.)* Model complete sentence responses, if necessary.

Use Role Playing ➤ Have two volunteers come forward. Have one child play a customer. Have the other child play a fruit seller. Give the customer 3 quarters. Give the fruit seller 20¢ and some apples or other play fruit. **The customer has 3 quarters. How much money is that?** *(75¢)* Write 75¢ on the board. **What does the customer need to know in order to buy apples?** *(The price of the apples; if he [or she] has enough money)* Tell the customer to tell the fruit seller, "I would like to buy these apples." Have the customer give the fruit seller the 3 quarters, and have the seller hand over the apples and 20 cents.

Did the customer have enough money? *(Yes)* **There was change or money left over. How much change was there?** *(20¢)* **How can we find out the price of the apples?** *(Subtract the change from the money the customer gave to the fruit seller. Subtract 20¢ from 75¢.)* Have the customer and the seller record 75¢ − 20¢ = 55¢ on the board. **What was the price of the apples?** *(55¢)*

Using Addition to Check Subtraction

USE WITH LESSON 6-7

ACTIVATE PRIOR KNOWLEDGE/BUILD BACKGROUND; EXTEND LANGUAGE

Objective Relate addition to subtraction by using one operation to check the other.

Materials *(per child)* 7 two-color counters

ESL Strategies **Use before** LEARN 🕐 15 MIN

Connect to Prior Knowledge of Math ➤ Give each child 7 counters. Demonstrate the subtraction fact $7 - 2 = 5$ with counters. Have children do it with you. **After you subtract 2 counters from 7 counters, how many do you have left?** *(5)* **How can you check to see if you subtracted correctly?** *(Add counters)* **Add the counters together again to find out if they equal 7. What two numbers would you add?** *(5 and 2)* **You started with 7 counters. When you check your subtraction by adding you should end up with the amount you had at the beginning.** Write $7 - 2 = 5$ and $5 + 2 = 7$ on the board. **Do you remember this?** Point to the fact family on the board. **What is this?** *(A fact family)* **What do you know about the number sentences that are in the same fact family?** *(Each number sentence has the same numbers.)* **Fact families show that you can use addition to check subtraction.**

Have Students Report Back Orally ➤ Write $96 - 55$ in vertical form on the board. Have a child subtract and record the answer on the board. *(41)* **To check your work, add.** Write $41 + 55 = 96$ in vertical form on the board. **Use addition to check subtraction.** Organize children into several groups, and assign each group a two-digit subtraction problem. Have each group record the subtraction problem, check their answer by recording the addition problem from the same fact family, and present their work to the class.

Estimating Differences

USE WITH LESSON 6-8

ACCESS CONTENT

Objective Estimate a difference to the nearest ten and then use that estimate to check the reasonableness of an exact answer.

Materials Place-Value Mat A (Workmat 4); tens and ones models

Vocabulary Estimate

ESL Strategies **Use before** CHECK ✓ 🕐 10 MIN

Use Manipulatives ➤ Write this problem on the board: "There are 53 books on the top shelf in the library. There are 39 books on the bottom shelf. How many more books are there on the top shelf than on the bottom shelf?" Read the problem together with children.

Have a volunteer write $53 - 39$ in vertical form on the board. Read and work through the problem with children. Have children solve the problem using tens and ones models and Workmat 4. Invite children to share the answer. *(14)* Write the answer on the board to complete the equation.

Use ➤
Demonstration

You know how to <u>estimate</u> to see if addition makes sense. You can estimate to check whether your answer makes sense when you subtract too. To estimate, find the nearest ten. Draw a number line from 30 to 60 on the board. Point to 53. **Is 53 closer to 50 or closer to 60?** *(50)* Write 50 on the board next to 53. **Is 39 closer to 30 or closer to 40?** *(40)* Write 40 on the board next to 39. **Let's subtract. What is 50 − 40?** *(10)* Write 10 on the board next to 14. **Is the estimate close to the exact answer?** *(Yes)* **Does the exact answer make sense?** *(Yes, 10 is close to 14.)*

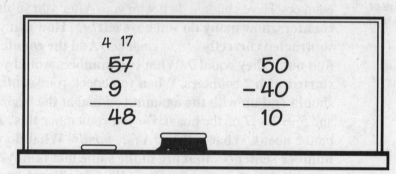

Ways to Subtract

ACCESS CONTENT/EXTEND LANGUAGE

Objective Choose an appropriate method for subtracting.

Materials *(all per pair)* Connecting cubes; Hundred Chart (Workmat 6); calculator

ESL Strategies

Use before **LEARN**

🕐 15 MIN

Use ➤
Demonstration

Write 42 − 23 on the board. Have two volunteers help you use connecting cubes to solve the problem. *(19)* Write the answer on the board. **We used cubes to subtract.** Write "cubes" on the board. **There are other ways to subtract. Who can name another way to find the answer to this problem?** *(Paper and pencil, mental math, calculator)* As children name the different ways to subtract, write them on the board. Then write the subtraction problem 81 − 57 on the board. Point to the phrase "paper and pencil." **How do you use paper and pencil to subtract 57 from 81?** Have a volunteer demonstrate on the board how to use the standard algorithm to regroup with paper and pencil. Repeat the activity for "mental math" and "calculator."

Have Students ➤
Report Back
Orally

Divide the class into pairs. Give each pair Workmat 6 with connecting cubes, paper, pencils, and a calculator. Write on the board, "34 dolphins were playing. 20 left to go find food. How many dolphins were left?" Read the problem aloud. **Work with your partner to solve this subtraction problem. Decide together which of the four ways you want to use to solve**

the problem. Let the pairs finish working through the problem. **How many dolphins were left playing?** *(14 dolphins were left playing.)* **Which way did you use to subtract?** Prompt children to answer in this format: "We used [name of method] to subtract." Have a child from each pair present to the class the steps they followed to find the solution.

Problem-Solving Skill: Extra Information

EXTEND LANGUAGE; ACCESS CONTENT

Objective Solve two-digit addition and subtraction problems after identifying and eliminating extra information.

Vocabulary Information

ESL Strategies   *Use before* **LEARN**   🕐 10–15 MIN

Focus on Meaning ➤ **The word <u>information</u> means facts or data about something. Can all information help you to solve a problem? Why or why not?** *(No, the information could be about something else.)* **Sometimes, you have to choose what information you need.**

Expand Student Responses ➤ Write this problem on the board: "Jose ate 2 apples for breakfast. Before lunch, he ate 2 oranges, and he had 2 bananas during lunch. In the afternoon he ate 1 apple. How many apples did Jose eat?" Read the problem aloud.

Point to the sentences on the board. **In this problem there is some information you do not need.** Repeat each sentence. Have a child come forward. **What are you trying to find?** *(The number of apples Jose ate)* **What information do you not need to find the answer?** *(The number of oranges and bananas)* **Why?** *(The question asks about apples.)* Have a second volunteer come forward and cross out the sentence about oranges and bananas. Then ask a third volunteer to solve the problem. **How many apples did Jose eat?** *(3)*

Problem-Solving Applications:
Here Kitty, Kitty!

EXTEND LANGUAGE

Objective Review and apply key concepts, skills, and strategies learned in this and previous chapters.

Materials *(per child)* Journal

ESL Strategies

Use after LEARN

🕐 15 MIN

Have Students ➤
Create Test Items

Divide the class into pairs. With their partners, have children read aloud the Writing in Math subtraction story they wrote about lions in their Journals. Have them write the subtraction problem number sentences they find in each other's stories.

Have two volunteers come forward to write the subtraction problems they found on the board. Using these problems, have the class identify ways they might find the differences. Then have children check the answers, based on what they have learned from this chapter. Continue the activity by inviting more volunteers to the board.

Flat Surfaces, Vertices, and Edges

ACTIVATE PRIOR KNOWLEDGE/BUILD BACKGROUND; EXTEND LANGUAGE

Objective Identify solid figures (cone, cube, cylinder, pyramid, rectangular prism, and sphere) and count their flat surfaces, vertices, and edges.

Materials Solid Figure and Plane Shape Cards (Teaching Tools 28 and 29)

ESL Strategies *Use before* **CHECK** ✓   🕐 10–15 MIN

Connect to Prior Experiences ➤ Divide the class into groups of four. Select solid figure cards that are part of this lesson, and distribute them to the groups. Have one child flash the figure cards one at a time to his or her group members. Have the others in the group first name the figure and then name some objects that have that shape. Have one volunteer in each group record the list.

Have Students Report Back Orally ➤ Repeat the activity with other cards. Each group should tally the number of objects that have been written down for each shape. Write a chart on the board showing each group's tally. If necessary, review with children how to tally the objects in their list.

Ask a volunteer from the group to come forward and report on the objects on their list. Have the other groups compare their lists and suggest additions.

Relating Plane Shapes to Solid Figures

ACCESS CONTENT; EXTEND LANGUAGE

Objective Match a geometric solid to an outline of one of its flat surfaces and match that flat surface to a plane shape.

Materials *(per pair)* Solid Figure and Plane Shape Cards (Teaching Tools 28 and 29)

Vocabulary Plane shapes

ESL Strategies *Use before* **CHECK** ✓   🕐 10–15 MIN

Use Small-Group Interactions ➤ Have the class work in pairs. Distribute solid-figure and plane-shape cards to each pair. Ask one child in each pair to flip over a card. **Is this a <u>plane shape</u> or a solid figure?** If it is a plane shape, ask the other child to write down the names of solid figures he or she can think of that have that plane shape as a face. If it is a solid figure, ask the child to write down the names of all the plane shapes he or she can find in the faces of the figure. If some children are not ready to write the words, have them draw the shapes.

Have pairs continue the activity with the other cards, switching roles each time. Ask a pair to come forward and write their answers on the board. Have them draw the shapes of the plane figures next to the matching word. Assist children with spelling as needed while focusing on praising them for finding correct answers.

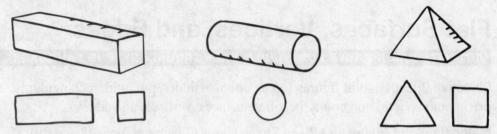

Problem-Solving Skill:
Use Data from a Picture

USE WITH LESSON
7-3

ACTIVATE PRIOR KNOWLEDGE/BUILD BACKGROUND; EXTEND LANGUAGE

Objective Solve problems by matching solid figures with their two-dimensional nets.

Materials Cone Net; Cylinder Net; Square Pyramid Net; Rectangular Prism Net (Teaching Tools 23–26)

Vocabulary Net

ESL Strategies ‖ *Use before* **LEARN**   ⏱ 10 MIN

Connect to Prior
Knowledge of
Math
➤ Draw a cube <u>net</u> on the board. **What shapes do you see in this drawing?** *(Squares, rectangles)* **How many of each?** *(6 squares, 2 rectangles. Some children may count as many as 10.)* Have volunteers point to each rectangle on the board until they are all counted.

Have Students
Report Back
in Writing
➤ Divide the class into four groups, and give each group one net. Ask children to write down all the plane figures they find in their net and to count how many. Have each group come forward, draw the shapes they have found, and label them. Assist children with spelling as needed.

Making New Shapes

USE WITH LESSON
7-4

ACCESS CONTENT

Objective Recognize and name trapezoids, parallelograms, and hexagons and identify the number of sides and angles in a polygon.

Materials *(per pair)* Pattern Blocks (Teaching Tool 30)

Vocabulary Trapezoid

ESL Strategies ‖ *Use before* **CHECK**   ⏱ 10 MIN

Use Manipulatives ➤ Have the class work in pairs. Give each pair pattern blocks. Give one partner a piece of paper with an illustration of a triangle that is pointed downward and is made out of two pattern blocks: a red <u>trapezoid</u> block and a green triangle block. **Don't show this drawing to your partner. You are going to**

explain to your partner how to make the shape shown on the paper.
Write on the board the following sentences: "Take a (color) (shape) block and a (color) (shape) block. Put the first block (on top of, under, next to) the second block." Read the sentences to children and explain that they have to replace the words in parentheses with the right words. **Let's try one.** Ask one child to repeat after you, and ask his or her partner to move the blocks according to the instructions. Point to the sentences on the board. **Take a *green triangle* block and a *red trapezoid* block. Put the *green triangle* block *under* the *red trapezoid* block. You should have one big green-and-red triangle.** Rotate among the pairs and help children as needed.

Have partners switch roles. Hand the child giving instructions a piece of paper illustrated with a red trapezoid, its wide side facing up, topped by two green triangles that are pointed upward. Have children with the illustration use the sentences on the board to help their partners form the correct shape.

Congruence

EXTEND LANGUAGE; ACCESS CONTENT

Objective Identify and create congruent figures.

Materials Two large (8-inch) paper plates; two small (6-inch) paper plates; rectangular piece of construction paper

Vocabulary Congruent

ESL Strategies *Use before* **LEARN** ◔ 10–15 MIN

Focus on Meaning ➤ Hold up one large paper plate. **What shape is this?** *(Circle)* Hold up the other large paper plate. **Is this the same shape?** *(Yes)* Have a volunteer come forward. Have the volunteer place one paper plate on top of the other. **Are the plates the same size?** *(Yes)* Now hold up one small paper plate. **What shape is this?** *(Circle)* **Are all three plates the same shape?** *(Yes)* Have the volunteer put the small plate on top of one of the large plates. **Are the plates all the same size?** *(No)* **Some things have the same shape, but they are not the same size.** Have the volunteer place the two large plates on top of each other, and the two small plates on top of each other. **When two figures have the same shape and are the same size, they are <u>congruent</u>.** Write "congruent" on the board.

Use ➤ Hold up a paper plate and a rectangular piece of construction paper. Place the
Demonstration plate on top of the construction paper. **Are these figures congruent?** *(No)* **How can you tell?** *(One is a rectangle and one is a circle; they are not the same shape and size.)*

Slides, Flips, and Turns

ACCESS CONTENT

USE WITH LESSON 7-6

Objective Perform a slide, flip, or turn on an object and identify the resulting orientation.

Materials Pattern Blocks (Teaching Tool 30)

Vocabulary Slide, flip, turn

ESL Strategies | ***Use before*** **LEARN** | 🕐 10–15 MIN

Use ➤ Demonstration

Give each child a pattern block. Demonstrate the words <u>slide</u>, <u>flip</u>, and <u>turn</u> using a pattern block, having children follow along with their own pattern blocks.

Use Total ➤ Physical Response

Let's play a game. I will say slide, flip, or turn. You will follow the instruction using pattern blocks. Stand up. Have children hold their pattern blocks in front of them. **When I say** *slide,* **slide your feet forward.** Demonstrate by sliding your feet forward and then practicing with children. **When I say** *turn,* **turn around in a circle.** Demonstrate by turning around in a circle and then practicing with children. **And when I say** *flip,* **stand in place and flip your block over.** Demonstrate by flipping your block over in your hands as you stand still. Practice flipping with children.

Play the game. Be sure children understand the directions for each word as you play.

Symmetry

ACCESS CONTENT

USE WITH LESSON 7-7

Objective Identify and create symmetrical shapes.

Materials Picture of a butterfly

Vocabulary Line of symmetry

Use Pictures ➤ **Symmetry means an object or image has two matching parts.** Show a picture of a butterfly with symmetrical wing designs. **Look at the butterfly. Does it show symmetry?** *(Yes)* **How do you know?** *(The size and shape of the butterfly's wings are the same.)* **Can you think of other examples of symmetry?** *(Valentine heart; maple leaf)*

Use ➤ Write a large 8 on the board. Then draw a vertical line down the middle.
Demonstration

Point to the line. **This is a** line of symmetry. **Do you see how the parts here** (point to the left side) **and here** (point to the right side) **are the same?** Erase the right side. **When objects are symmetrical, you can copy one side to make the other side.** Redraw the right side of the 8, pointing out its symmetrical relation to the left side. Clarify that when you copy one side of a figure to show symmetry, you flip, or turn over, that part onto the other side.

Write another 8 beside the first and draw a vertical line off-center, so that it divides the 8 asymmetrically. Point to this line. **Is this a line of symmetry?** *(No)* **Why?** *(The two parts do not match.)*

Problem-Solving Strategy: Use Logical Reasoning

USE WITH LESSON
7-8

ACCESS PRIOR KNOWLEDGE/BUILD BACKGROUND; ACCESS CONTENT

Objective Solve a problem by using logical reasoning.

Connect to Prior ➤ **What is a clue?** *(Information that helps you answer a question; accept all*
Knowledge of *reasonable answers)* **How would you find clues in a word problem?** *(Look*
Language *for words and numbers that tell important information.)*

Use Small-Group ➤ Organize the class into groups of four. Have children talk about their answers
Interactions to the following questions, and write down some ideas. **What kinds of information might you get from clues?** *(What is important; what is different about one part of the problem; what you don't need to solve the problem; whether to add or subtract; and so on)* **Can you think of two ways you can use clues to help you answer problems?** *(Encourage and accept all reasonable answers.)*

Equal Parts

USE WITH LESSON 7-9

ACCESS CONTENT; EXTEND LANGUAGE

Objective Determine whether a shape has been divided into equal or unequal parts; identify halves, thirds, and fourths.

Materials *(per child)* 2 square pieces of paper measuring 6 in. across; ruler

Vocabulary Equal, halves, thirds, fourths

ESL Strategies *Use before* **LEARN**

⏱ 10–15 MIN

Use **>** Demonstration

Give each child a square piece of paper. **Fold your paper in half.** Demonstrate by holding up a piece of paper and folding the left side over to the right side, creating a crease down the middle. Unfold the paper to display the whole sheet. **Now unfold your paper. Draw a line over the crease, or the line that shows the fold.** Demonstrate this. **How many parts are there now?** *(2)* **Are they both the same size?** *(Yes)* **When 2 parts are the same size, they are <u>equal</u>. 2 equal parts of one figure or object are called <u>halves</u>.**

Focus on Meaning **>**

Have children take the same piece of paper and fold it top over the bottom, so that when the sheet is opened, there are 4 equal squares. **Unfold your paper. Draw a line over the new crease. Now how many parts are there?** *(4)* **Are they equal?** *(Yes)* **4 equal parts of 1 figure or object are called <u>fourths</u>.**

Give each child the second square piece of paper. Using a ruler, show how to divide the paper lengthwise into three 2-inch parts. **How many parts are there?** *(3)* **Are they all equal?** *(Yes)* **3 equal parts of 1 figure or object are called <u>thirds</u>.**

Unit Fractions

USE WITH LESSON 7-10

ACCESS CONTENT

Objective Identify and show a unit fraction of a region.

Materials *(per child)* Two 12-inch strips of construction paper; *(per pair)* four 12-in. strips of construction paper, with 2 strips having a line drawn one-third (4 inch) of the way from the edge

Vocabulary Fraction

ESL Strategies *Use before* **LEARN**

⏱ 15 MIN

Use **>** Demonstration

Give each child two rectangular strips of construction paper. Hold up one strip. **This is a whole piece of paper.** Have students fold their strip into 2 equal parts and cut the paper at the fold. **How many parts are there now?** *(2)* **Are they the same size?** *(Yes)* **What do we call 2 equal parts?** *(Halves)* Hold up another strip. **This is a whole piece of paper.** Have students fold their second strip into unequal parts and cut the paper at the fold. **How many** parts are there now? *(2)* **Are they the same size?** *(No)* **When parts are not the same size, they are unequal. Are these parts halves?** *(No)*

Write $\frac{1}{2}$ and "one half" on the board. Point to the <u>fraction</u>. **The bottom number tells how many equal parts one figure or object has in all. How many equal parts does this fraction show in all?** *(2)* Hold up the equal parts of the strip. **What are 2 equal parts called?** *(Halves)* **The top number shows how many of the equal parts there are. How many parts of the strip do you see here?** *(1)* **This part shows $\frac{1}{2}$ of the strip.** Point to the numerator as you say "one" and point to the denominator as you say "half." Invite students to repeat "one half" after you.

Use Small-Group ➤ Interactions

Put children into pairs. Distribute two more strips of construction paper to each pair and have them repeat the activity for 4 equal parts to ensure children know how to make fourths. Then distribute the strips that have a line drawn on them four inches (one third) from the left end. Repeat the activity, demonstrating thirds for them.

Non-Unit Fractions

ACCESS CONTENT

Objective Identify and show any fraction of a region.

Materials *(per child)* Crayon; paper with drawing of rectangle divided into 8 equal parts

ESL Strategies **Use before** **LEARN**   ⏱ 10 MIN

Use ➤ Demonstration

Draw a circle on the board and divide it into 4 equal parts. **How many equal parts are there in all?** *(4)* Write 4 on the board. Shade in 1 of the sectors. **How may parts are shaded?** *(1)* **1 of the 4 parts is shaded. How can I write a fraction to show this?** *(Write 1 on the top and 4 on the bottom.)* Write $\frac{1}{4}$ on the board. Shade in another sector. **Now how many parts are shaded?** *(2)* **What fraction shows this?** *($\frac{2}{4}$)* Write $\frac{2}{4}$ on the board. Shade in a third sector. **Now how many parts are shaded?** *(3)* **What fraction shows this?** *($\frac{3}{4}$)* Write $\frac{3}{4}$ on the board.

Use Pictures ➤

Give each child a crayon and a piece of paper with a drawing of a rectangle divided into 8 equal parts. **How many equal parts are there?** *(8)* **Color in 1 part. How many parts are shaded?** *(1)* **What fraction shows that 1 part of 8 is shaded?** *($\frac{1}{8}$)* Tell children to write the fraction on their paper. **Color in 2 more parts. How many parts are shaded now?** *(3)* **What is the fraction that shows that 3 of the 8 parts are shaded?** *($\frac{3}{8}$)* Continue having children shade in parts, and ask them to write the appropriate fractions on their papers.

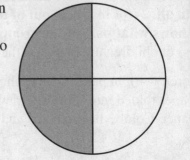
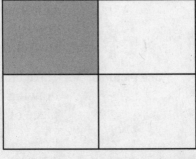

Estimating Fractions

ACTIVATE PRIOR KNOWLEDGE/BUILD BACKGROUND; EXTEND LANGUAGE

Objective Estimate the fraction for a given part of a region.

Vocabulary Estimate

ESL Strategies *Use before* **LEARN** 🕐 10–15 MIN

Connect to Prior
Knowledge of
Math
➤ **You know that sometimes you don't need an exact answer. Remember that when you buy things in a store, sometimes you just want to know you have enough money. How can you figure out whether you have enough?** (*Estimate*)

Suppose I am making pancakes and need a third of a carton of milk. How can I tell whether I have enough milk left in my carton? (*Mentally divide the carton into thirds; look to see if there is more than a third in the carton.*) **I can estimate the fraction.**

Have Students
Create Test Items
➤ Divide the class into small groups. Have each child write short-form answers to the following questions. **When else would it be good to estimate fractions?** (*Dividing food among friends; estimating time or parts of an hour; and so on*) **Write an estimating fraction problem for your partners. Draw a picture that will help them answer it. Take turns asking and answering one another's problems.** Work individually with English language learners to help them articulate and write their fraction problem. Be sure to also help them with spelling and grammar.

Fractions of a Set

ACCESS CONTENT

Objective Identify and show fractions of a set of objects.

Materials (*per pair*) 2 sheets of large drawing paper folded into quarters; crayons

ESL Strategies *Use before* **LEARN** 🕐 10 MIN

Use
Demonstration
➤ Ask 5 volunteers to come forward. Be sure that there is more than 1 boy and more than 1 girl. **How many children in all are standing in front of the class?** (*5 children*) Write "5 children" on the board. **How many children in the group are boys?** Write the number of boys on the board. **There are 5 children in all. 2** (for instance) **out of the 5 in the group are boys. What fraction shows what part of the group is made up of boys?** ($\frac{2}{5}$) Write "$\frac{2}{5}$ (two-fifths) of children are boys" on the board.

Use Pictures ➤ Have children work in pairs. Give each pair crayons and a large sheet of drawing paper folded into fourths. Draw 4 balloons on the board or large piece of paper. Color 3 balloons red and 1 balloon blue. Have one child in each pair make the same drawing in one of the fourths of the drawing paper. **How many balloons are there in all?** *(4 balloons)* Write "4 balloons in all" on the board or on a sheet of paper. Have the other child in the pair copy what you have written in the next quarter of the paper. **How many balloons are red?** *(3 balloons)* Write "3 balloons are red" on the board or paper. Ask the other child to copy what you have written in another quarter of the paper. **What fraction of the balloons is red?** *($\frac{3}{4}$)* Write the fraction on the board. Have each pair copy the fraction in the last quarter on their paper.

Give each pair another sheet of drawing paper folded into fourths, and repeat the activity to show the fraction of blue balloons.

Problem-Solving Applications: Under the Sea

USE WITH LESSON 7-14

EXTEND LANGUAGE

Objective Review and apply key concepts, skills, and strategies learned in this and previous chapters.

Materials Math journals

ESL Strategies *Use after*

Application

🕐 15 MIN

Group the class in pairs. Have each child look at his or her partner's drawing of a seashell from the Writing in Math exercise and read the explanation. Ask children to write answers to the following questions in their journals after discussing them with their partners. **Do you agree that the shell is symmetric? Do you agree with your partner's explanation? Why?** Try to pair English language learners with students who are fluent in English.

Draw a line of symmetry on your partner's seashell. What equal part of the shell does this make? Is this the only line of symmetry you can draw? If you can draw another line of symmetry, what equal part of the shell does this make? Is the shell still symmetric if you slide it? If you flip it? If you turn it?

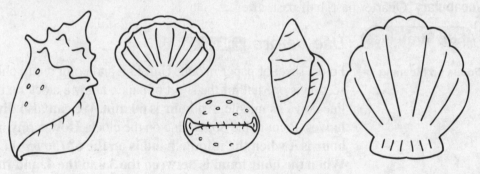

Telling Time to Five Minutes

USE WITH LESSON
8-1

EXTEND LANGUAGE; ACCESS CONTENT

Objective Tell time to five-minute intervals.

Materials *(per group)* Clock Face (Teaching Tool 34)

Vocabulary Hour hand, minute hand, hour

ESL Strategies *Use before* **LEARN**

 10 MIN

Focus on Meaning ➤ Discuss with children that they can use their hands to help express themselves. Then discuss how the hands of a clock express the time. **The smaller hand, the** <u>hour hand</u>**, points to the** <u>hour</u>**. The larger hand, the** <u>minute hand</u>**, points to the minute.** Explain that the hour hand is read before the minute hand.

Use Small-Group ➤ Have children work in small groups. Give each group a clock face. On a
Interactions clock face, demonstrate how the minute hand moves from 12 clockwise to 12 during the course of an hour. Then repeat the demonstration, this time slowly skip counting every 5 min until you get to 60 min. Quiz children on how many minutes after the hour it is when the minute hand is on a five-minute interval. For example, ask, **How many minutes after the hour is it when the minute hand is on 3?** *(15 min)* Then have children tell time by asking such questions as, **What time is it when the hour hand is between the 7 and 8 and the minute hand is on 4?** *(7:20)*

Telling Time After the Hour

USE WITH LESSON
8-2

EXTEND LANGUAGE; ACCESS CONTENT

Objective Tell time after the hour.

Vocabulary Quarter past, half past, after

ESL Strategies *Use before* **CHECK** ✓

10–15 MIN

Focus on Meaning ➤ Fold a sheet of paper in half. Unfold it and point out to children that each section is one half of the sheet of paper. Draw a clock on the board with a dotted line down its middle. **An hour is 60 min. We can also divide an hour into halves.** Point to the dotted line on the clock. **How many minutes** <u>after</u> **the hour is it when the minute hand is on the 6?** *(30 min)* **Look at the clock. When the hour hand is between the 3 and the 4, and the minute hand is on the 6, it is 3:30. We can also say that it is** <u>half past</u> **three or 30 min after three.** Write the three different ways to say the time on the board. Clarify for children that the word *half* is used only when the minute hand is on the 6.

Take the piece of paper already folded in half and fold it in half again.

Explain that each section of the paper is one fourth, or a quarter, of the sheet of paper. Draw a dotted line across the middle of the clock on the board. **We can also divide an hour into quarters. What numbers does the minute hand point to when each quarter of an hour ends?** *(3, 6, 9, and 12)*

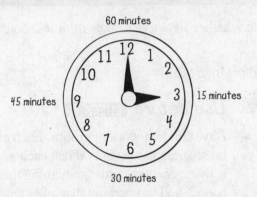

Use
Demonstration ➤ Show 12:00 on the clock. Then move the minute hand so that it points to 3. **It is now 12:15, or <u>quarter past</u> twelve. Show 1:00. Then move the minute hand so that it points to 3. What time is it?** *(1:15, or 15 min after one, or quarter past one)* Encourage children to tell the time in different ways. Move the minute hand so that it points to 6. **What time is it?** *(1:30, or 30 min after one, or half past one)* Move the minute hand so that it points to 9. **What time is it?** *(1:45, or 45 min after one, or 45 min past one)*

Have children draw clocks and write different times with the minute hand on the 3, 6, or 9.

Telling Time Before the Hour

USE WITH LESSON
8-3

ACTIVATE PRIOR KNOWLEDGE/BUILD BACKGROUND

Objective Tell time before the hour.

Vocabulary Before, quarter to

ESL Strategies ***Use before*** CHECK ✓ ⏱ 5–10 MIN

Connect to Prior
Knowledge of
Math ➤ Discuss with children that to tell time <u>before</u> the hour, you find how many minutes there are until the next hour. Draw a clock on the board that shows 10:50. Have children count aloud with you as you skip count by 5-min intervals from 12 back to 10. **How many minutes are there between 10:50 and 11:00?** *(10 min)* **We can say that 10:50 is 10 min before 11:00.**

Show 9:15 on the clock. **What else can you call 9:15?** *(Sample answers: Quarter past 9:00, 15 min after 9:00)* Show 9:45 on the clock. **What time is it on the clock?** *(Sample answers: 9:45, 45 min after 9:00, 45 min past 9:00)* **What is the next hour?** *(10:00)* **How many minutes are there until 10:00?** *(15 min)* **We can also say that 9:45 is <u>quarter to</u> 10:00. What does quarter to 10:00 mean?** *(There is a quarter hour, or 15 min, before 10:00.)* Show other times with the clock on the board, and have children tell the time in different ways.

Estimating Time

Objective Estimate whether an activity takes minutes, hours, or days to complete.

Materials *(per group)* Index cards

ESL Strategies

Use before CHECK ✓

⏱ 5 MIN

Use Small-Group ➤
Interactions

Have children work in groups. Each child writes "minutes," "hours," and "days" on separate index cards. Then each group member writes the name of an activity, one to a card: "something that takes minutes," "something that takes hours," and "something that takes days." Have groups exchange their activity cards with another group. One group member states the activity on one of the cards that the group received. The other group members raise either their minutes, hours, or days card to show how long they estimate the activity would take. For example, if the activity card says "play soccer," children should raise their hours card. If children disagree on their estimates, have the group discuss the activity. Have children switch roles and repeat for the other activity cards. Walk around the room and ask groups how many of each unit of time the activity takes. For "play soccer," children might say that it takes one or two hours.

Elapsed Time

Objective Determine the amount of time that passes between the start of an event and the end of an event, and determine the ending time when given the elapsed time.

Materials *(per child)* Clock Face (Teaching Tool 34)

ESL Strategies

Use before LEARN

⏱ 10 MIN

Give Frequent ➤
Feedback

Display 6:00 on a clock. **Yesterday I saw a movie. It started at six o'clock.** Display 8:00 on another clock. **The movie ended at eight o'clock. How long was the movie?** *(2 hours)* Ask a volunteer to explain how he or she knew that the movie was 2 hours long. *(By counting on the hours from 6:00 to 8:00)* **A 2-hour movie started at seven o'clock. When did it end?** *(9:00)* **How do you know the movie ended at nine?** *(I counted on from seven to nine.)*

Have Students Report Back in Writing ➤ Distribute clock faces to children. Have children write down what they have done today up to this point, such as get ready for school, eat breakfast, or take the bus to school. For each activity, they should note the elapsed time. Have children include drawings of clocks showing the time at the beginning and end of each activity.

Start   End

Got ready for school 30 minutes.

A.M. and P.M.

USE WITH LESSON 8-6

EXTEND LANGUAGE

Objective Determine whether events occur in the A.M. or P.M. hours.

Materials Clock Face (Teaching Tool 34)

Vocabulary Midnight, A.M., P.M.

ESL Strategies   *Use before* **LEARN**   🕐 5–10 MIN

Focus on Use ➤ **There are 24 hours in one day, which can be divided into two 12-hour sections. Each day starts at <u>midnight</u>. Show 12:00 on a clock face.** *Midnight is short for the middle of the night.* **What do you do in the middle of the night?** *(Sample answer: Sleep)* Ask a volunteer what time he or she woke up, for example, eight o'clock. **You can say that you woke up at 8:00 A.M.** Explain that the A.M. hours last from midnight until noon.

Noon is the start of the P.M. hours. The P.M. hours last from noon until midnight. Have children make three lists, one for things that they do in both parts of the day, one for things that they do only in the A.M., and one for things that they do only in the P.M.

Brush teeth	Wake up		Go to sleep
Go to school	Get ready for school		Do homework
Eat lunch	Eat breakfast		Eat dinner

Using a Calendar

ACCESS CONTENT

Objective Complete, read, and use a calendar.

Materials *(per group)* Calendar (Teaching Tool 11)

Vocabulary Calendar

ESL Strategies | *Use before* **LEARN** | 🕐 10 MIN

Use Small-Group Interactions ➤ Ask a volunteer for today's date. Ask another volunteer what each part of the date means. *(Month, day, year)* Display the classroom <u>calendar</u> and point to today's date. Have children work in small groups. Distribute a calendar to each group. Tell children where today's date goes on the calendar. **Today is (day of the week), the (ordinal number) of the month.** Have groups fill in the information for the rest of the month. Help children identify the first and last day of the month, if necessary.

Use Peer Questioning ➤ When the calendars have been completed, have group members take turns quizzing one another. Instruct them to ask what day of the week a certain date is and which day of the week comes before or after the chosen day. Then have children quiz each other about the order of the months and the number of days in each month.

What day is the fourth Friday in March?

Equivalent Times

EXTEND LANGUAGE; ACTIVATE PRIOR KNOWLEDGE/BUILD BACKGROUND

Objective Solve problems involving equivalent times.

Materials *(per pair)* 12 index cards

Vocabulary Equivalent

ESL Strategies | *Use before* **LEARN** | 🕐 10 MIN

Focus on Meaning ➤ Write "<u>equivalent</u>" on the board. **What word is similar to *equivalent*?** *(Equal)* **How have you used the word *equal* in math?** *(Sample answer: To describe two parts that are the same) Equivalent* means the same.

Divide the class into pairs. Distribute 12 index cards to each pair. Write the following words on the board and have pairs copy the words onto their index cards: "Quarter Hour," "Half Hour," "Hour," "Day," "Week," "Month," "15 minutes," "30 minutes," "60 minutes," "24 hours," "7 days," "30 days."

Have pairs mix up their cards and spread them out facedown. In turns, have partners turn over two cards. If the cards show equivalent times, the child keeps the cards. Otherwise the child turns the cards facedown again. Walk around the room asking how pairs know two times are equivalent or not. The game ends when all of the cards have been taken.

Problem-Solving Strategy: Make a Table

USE WITH LESSON
8-9

ACCESS CONTENT

Objective Solve a problem by making a table.

ESL Strategies

Use before LEARN

🕐 10–15 MIN

Use ➤
Demonstration

Explain to children that one way to organize information is to make a table. **Suppose we want to know about the hair color of the children in our class. We can make a table to show this information.** Make a table on the board like the one below.

Hair Color	Blond	Brown	Red	Black
Number of Children				

Demonstrate how a tally table works. Mark a tally below the appropriate heading for each child's hair color. When you have finished, ask the following questions: **How many children have blond hair? How many children have red hair? How many children have brown hair? How many children have black hair? How many children are in the class?** *(Answers for the questions will vary.)* Remind children that each tally stands for one child.

Use Small-Group ➤
Interactions

Divide the class into groups of three or four. Have children come up with other questions that can be answered using the information in the table. *(Sample answer: How many more children have brown hair than red hair?)* Invite volunteers from each group to share their questions with the class. Ask children how they might answer the questions. *(Sample answer: Subtract the number of children with red hair from the number of children with brown hair.)*

Recording Data from a Survey

USE WITH LESSON
8-10

Objective Collect and analyze data that have been gathered using a survey.

Vocabulary Survey, data

ESL Strategies | *Use before* **LEARN** | ⏱ 10–15 MIN

Use → Explain to children that a <u>survey</u> is a group of questions asked to collect <u>data</u>,
Demonstration   or information. **We are going to conduct a survey on your favorite lunch food. We can make a table to show this information.** Make a two-column table on the board like the one below.

What is your favorite lunch food?

Food	Number
Hamburgers	
Pizza	
Tacos	
Spaghetti	

Ask each child for his or her favorite lunch food and mark a tally where appropriate. When every member of the class has responded, ask the following questions: **What did most children say is their favorite lunch food? Which lunch food was the favorite of the least number of children? How many more children like pizza than tacos?** (*Answers for the questions will vary.*)

Use Small-Group → Divide the class into groups of three or four. Have children think of other
Interactions   survey questions that can be answered using the information in the table. (*Sample answer: What is your favorite color?*) Invite volunteers from each group to share their questions with the class. Ask the class to answer those questions.

Using a Venn Diagram

USE WITH LESSON
8-11

Objective Collect, record, and analyze data using a Venn diagram.

Materials (*per child*) Two-color counters

Vocabulary Venn diagram

Use Manipulatives ➤ Distribute two-color counters to children. **I have given each of you two-color counters.** Hold up a counter and say, **One side of each counter is red, and the other side is yellow. I want you to do one of these things: show only red counters, show only yellow counters, or show some red and some yellow counters.**

Now we are going to make a <u>Venn diagram</u>**. A Venn diagram shows three types of data, or information. It shows how many things belong to one group, how many belong to another, and how many belong to both groups.** Draw a Venn diagram on the board. Label the circles "I have red," "I have yellow," and "I have both."

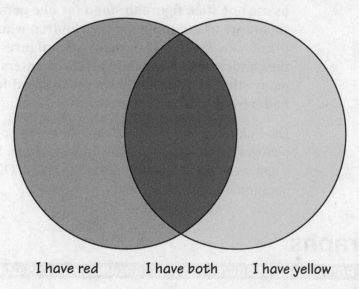

I have red   I have both   I have yellow

Use Graphic Organizers ➤ Ask each child if he or she has red counters, only yellow counters, or both red and yellow counters. Write the name of each child in the appropriate circle. When the diagram has been completed, ask the following questions: **How can you find how many children have red counters?** *(Add the number of names that have red counters and red and yellow counters.)* **How many children have red counters?** *(Answers will vary.)* **How can you find how many children have yellow counters?** *(Add the number of names that have yellow counters and red and yellow counters.)* **How many children have yellow counters?** *(Answers will vary.)* **How can you find how many children have red and yellow counters?** *(Count the names in the middle circle.)* **How many children have red and yellow counters?** *(Answers will vary.)* Record the data from this lesson to use for the activity in Lesson 8-12.

Pictographs

USE WITH LESSON
8-12

EXTEND LANGUAGE; ACCESS CONTENT

Objective Create and analyze data using a pictograph.

Vocabulary Pictograph

Use before LEARN ⏱ 10 MIN

Focus on Meaning ➤ Write the word "pictograph" on the board and read it aloud. Underline *graph* in the word *pictograph*. **What is a graph?** *(Sample answer: A set of columns and rows that shows information, or data)* **What are the first four letters at the beginning of the word *pictograph*?** *(Pict)* Circle *pict* in *pictograph*. **What is another word that starts with *pict*?** *(Picture)* Explain that a pictograph is a graph that uses pictures to show information.

Use ➤
Demonstration
Use the data from Lesson 8-11 to create a pictograph on the board. Write the data for how many children have only red counters, how many have only yellow counters, and how many have red and yellow counters. Explain that a pictograph uses a symbol, or sign, to represent a certain number. **Let us use one stick figure to stand for one person. How many stick figures should we use to stand for the children who have only red counters?** *(Answers will vary.)* **How many stick figures should we use to stand for the children who have only yellow counters?** *(Answers will vary.)* **How many stick figures should we use to stand for the children who have both red and yellow counters?** *(Answers will vary.)*

Have children volunteer questions that can be answered by looking at the pictograph, such as how many more children have red counters than yellow counters. Write the questions on the board. Discuss with children how each question might be answered.

Bar Graphs

USE WITH LESSON
8-13

ACTIVATE PRIOR KNOWLEDGE/BUILD BACKGROUND; ACCESS CONTENT

Objective Create and analyze bar graphs.

Materials Counters; (per pair) grid paper

Vocabulary Bar graph

Use before CHECK ✓ ⏱ 5 MIN

Connect to Prior ➤
Knowledge of
Math
Write "bar graph" on the board and read it aloud. Underline the word *graph*. **What is a pictograph?** *(A graph that uses pictures to show information)* **What do you think a bar graph is?** *(A graph that uses bars to show information)* Explain that like a pictograph, a bar graph shows data that can be compared. **How do you read a pictograph?** *(Sample answer: Find what each symbol, or sign, stands for and count the number of symbols.)* Explain that the end of each bar in a bar graph corresponds to a number along the vertical axis. That is how you read a bar graph.

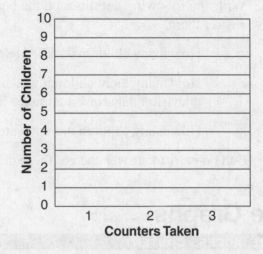

Counters Taken (x-axis)
Number of Children (y-axis)

Give Frequent
Feedback ➤ Ask children to take 1, 2, or 3 counters from a pile that you have created on a desk. Set up a tally table on the board, and ask each child how many counters he or she took. When the tally table is complete, divide the class into pairs and distribute grid paper. Draw an outline of a bar graph on the board.

Each pair should make a bar graph of the data from the tally table. Walk around the room and check on each pair's progress. **What does each bar stand for?** (*The number of children who took a certain number of counters*) **If (insert number) children took 1 counter, how many boxes should you use for your bar?** (*Answer should be the same as the number of children.*)

Line Plots

ACCESS CONTENT

USE WITH LESSON
8-14

Objective Create and analyze line plots.

Vocabulary Line plot

[ESL Strategies] ➤ *Use before* **CHECK** ✓   ⏱ 5 MIN

Use ➤
Demonstration
Have each child write the number of hours that they watched television last Sunday on scrap paper. Have children hand in their papers. **Let us construct a line plot of the number of hours that you watched television last Sunday.**

Have children draw the skeleton of a line plot as shown below. Read aloud the number written on each piece of paper. Children should record an *X* in the appropriate place to make their line plots.

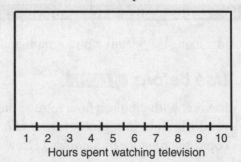

1 2 3 4 5 6 7 8 9 10
Hours spent watching television

| Use Small-Group Interactions | ➤ | Write the following questions on the board. Have children work in pairs to answer them. |

How many children watched television for 2 hours?

How many more children watched for (insert number) hours of television than (insert number) hours of television?

How many children did not watch any television at all?

Call on pairs to answer each of these questions. *(Answers will vary.)*

Coordinate Graphs

EXTEND LANGUAGE; ACCESS CONTENT

USE WITH LESSON 8-15

Objective Locate and name points on a coordinate grid.

Materials *(per child)* Grid paper

Vocabulary Ordered pair, coordinate graph

| **ESL Strategies** | ***Use before*** **LEARN** | 🕐 10 MIN |

| Focus on Meaning | ➤ | Write "<u>ordered pair</u>" on the board and read it aloud. **What does the word *order* mean?** *(Sample answers: To tell someone what to do; to arrange)* **In this lesson, the meaning of the word *order* that we will use is "to arrange." What is a pair?** *(A group of two things)* **What is an ordered pair?** *(Two numbers that are arranged)* **An ordered, or arranged, pair names a point on a graph. A graph that shows ordered pairs is called a <u>coordinate graph</u>.** |

| Use Small-Group Interactions | ➤ | Give children grid paper. Have them make 5-by-5 grids and label the bottom axis from A to E and the side axis from 1 to 5. **Remember that you read the label at the bottom of the graph first. Then you read the label on the side of the graph. So if a point is at D and at 2, the ordered pair that names the point is (D, 2).** Write "(D, 2)" on the board. Have each child draw a rectangle or square on his or her grid. Then have him or her write the ordered pairs naming the corner points. Walk around the room and check children's work. |

Problem-Solving Skill: Use Data from a Graph

ACTIVATE PRIOR KNOWLEDGE/BUILD BACKGROUND; EXTEND LANGUAGE

USE WITH LESSON 8-16

Objective Solve problems using data from a pictograph and a bar graph.

| **ESL Strategies** | ***Use before*** **LEARN** | 🕐 10–15 MIN |

| Connect to Prior Knowledge of Math | ➤ | Review with children how to read pictographs and bar graphs. **How do you read the data in a pictograph?** *(Find out what each picture stands for and count the number of pictures.)* Draw the following pictograph on the board. |

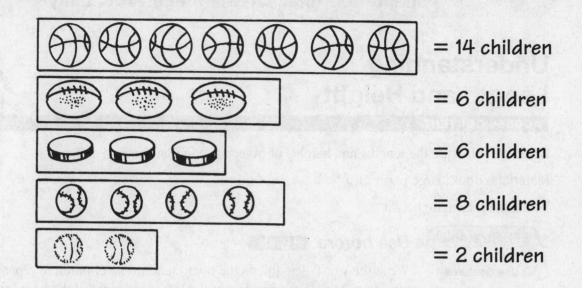

= 14 children

= 6 children

= 6 children

= 8 children

= 2 children

Have Students Create Test Items ➤ **If each ball stands for 2 children and there are 7 balls in the basketball row, how many children chose basketball as their favorite sport?** *(14 children)* **How did you find your answer?** *(I counted on by two 7 times.)* **How would a bar graph show the same data?** *(With a bar that ends at 14)* Remind children that a pictograph and a bar graph can show the same data in different ways.

Have children work in small groups to write other questions that can be answered using the pictograph. Write one of each group's questions on the board as a volunteer reads it to you. Assign each group's question to a different group. When children are finished, ask members of each group to explain how they got the answer to their assigned question.

Problem-Solving Applications: Fly, Butterfly, Fly

EXTEND LANGUAGE

USE WITH LESSON
8-17

Objective Review and apply key concepts, skills, and strategies learned in this and previous chapters.

ESL Strategies | *Use before* **LEARN**   🕐 15 MIN

Have Students Create Test Items ➤ Have children work in pairs. Have them read to each other the Writing in Math story that they wrote in their journals about caterpillars changing into butterflies. Then ask them to write in their journals any time-related questions that they found in their partners' stories.

Ask several volunteers to come up to the board and write a problem about time from the stories that they read. Ask children to identify how they would find the time or elapsed time and how they would check their answer for each question on the board, based on what they have learned from this chapter.

Understanding Length and Height

ACCESS CONTENT

USE WITH LESSON **9-1**

Objective Measure the lengths and heights of objects using nonstandard units.

Materials Book; large paper clip

Vocabulary Length, height

ESL Strategies ⎰ *Use before* LEARN

⏱ 10 MIN

Use Gestures ➤ Write the word "length" on the board, and invite children to repeat the word after you. Move your hand from the left to the right of the board to demonstrate that length is the measure of how long something is. **What are some other things you can measure the length of?** *(Sample answers: a wall, a box, and so on)* Then write the word "height" on the board and invite children to repeat the word after you. Move your hand from the top to the bottom of your desk to demonstrate that *height* is the measure of how tall something is. **What are some other things you can measure the height of?** *(Sample answers: a person, a building, and so on)*

Use Real Objects ➤ Ask a volunteer to stand beside you. Point from the child's head to his or her feet and explain that you want to measure the child's height. Use a large book to measure the child's height. Count aloud with children, saying, **One book, two books, three books, four books . . .** When you have finished measuring, repeat the number of books tall the child is, and write the measurement on the board. For example: **Five and a half books. (Child) is five and a half books tall. Is this (Child)'s length or height?** *(Height)* **How do you know?** *(Height measures how tall something is.)* Repeat the activity, using a large paper clip to measure the length of one of the volunteer's feet.

Inches and Feet

ACCESS CONTENT

Objective Estimate and measure the lengths or heights of objects in inches or feet, using a ruler.

Materials Ruler

Vocabulary Foot (ft), inch (in.), ruler

ESL Strategies | *Use before* **CHECK** | ⏱ 10 MIN

Use Gestures ➤ **I am going to ask some questions, and I would like everyone to show me the answers without speaking. About how long is a <u>foot</u>? This long?** Hold your hands out at full arm span. **This long?** Hold your hands very close together. Correct children's gestures without speaking by mirroring with your own, until all students have found a good estimated length for one foot. **About how long is an <u>inch</u>?** *(Check that children gesture with thumb and forefinger.)* **About how long is an average grown man's foot?** *(Check that children make the same gesture as for 1 foot.)* **About how long is an inchworm?** *(Check that children make the same gesture as for 1 inch.)*

Use ➤ Demonstration Invite volunteers to the front of the room to demonstrate for the class. **Show the class your estimate for two feet. How about three feet? About how long is two inches? Four inches?** Help each volunteer to arrive at a good estimate for each length, then have the class mirror the gestures with minimal speaking.

Draw a line about 6 inches long on the board. **About how long is this line? You can answer in words.** *(6 inches)* **Yes, that is a good estimate for the length of the line. How can we find the exact length of the line?** *(Measure it)* **Yes, we can use a <u>ruler</u> to measure the line.** Invite a volunteer to come to the front of the class and use the ruler. Make sure children understand that they need to start at the left edge of the ruler and measure to the end of the line. Repeat with different lengths.

Inches, Feet, and Yards

ACTIVATE PRIOR KNOWLEDGE/BUILD BACKGROUND

Objective Estimate and measure the lengths or heights of objects in inches, feet, or yards, using a ruler.

Materials Ruler; yardstick

Vocabulary Yardstick, yard (yd)

ESL Strategies

Use before LEARN ⏱ 10 MIN

Connect to Prior Experiences ➢ Display a ruler for the class. **This ruler measures up to 1 ft. How many inches are in 1 ft?** *(12 in.)* Display a yardstick for the class. **This is a yardstick. It measures up to 1 yard.** Compare the ruler to the yardstick. **How many feet do you think are in a yardstick?** *(3 ft)* Explain that we use the same process to measure with a yardstick as we do a ruler. **When do you think it is easier to measure things in yards than in feet or inches?** *(Sample answer: When you are measuring very large things)*

Use Brainstorming ➢ Write "inches," "feet," and "yards" on the board as heads for three separate columns. Point to "inches" and ask children to brainstorm items that can be measured in inches. List reasonable responses in the first column on the board. Point to feet and ask children to think of items that can be measured in feet. List these responses in the second column. Point to yards and have children brainstorm items that can be measured in yards. Write their responses in the third column. Pick one example of an item from each column that you have in the classroom. Demonstrate how to estimate the measurement and then measure the item using the indicated measurement.

For example, if children chose a pencil as an item to be measured in inches, say, **How many inches do you think this pencil is?** Record a child's estimate in inches on the board. Then ask, **How many inches is this pencil?** Have a volunteer measure the pencil with a ruler. Record the child's measurement on the board. Compare the estimate with the actual measurement. Repeat this demonstration twice more, using items from the feet and yards columns.

Centimeters and Meters

ACCESS CONTENT

Objective Estimate and measure lengths in centimeters and meters, using a centimeter ruler or a meterstick.

Materials Centimeter ruler; meterstick

Vocabulary Centimeter ruler, centimeter (cm), meterstick, meter (m)

ESL Strategies   *Use before* LEARN   10 MIN

Use ➤
Demonstration

Draw a horizontal line about 20 cm long on the board. **What unit of measure could you use to find the length of this line?** *(Inches)* Measure the line using the inch ruler and write "8 inches" under the line. Tell children that they could also use a <u>centimeter ruler</u> to measure the line. Demonstrate using a centimeter ruler, explaining that <u>centimeters</u> are smaller than inches. Explain that, like an inch ruler, they need to start at the left and measure until the end of the object. Next to the line, write "20 centimeters." Read aloud the measurement and invite children to repeat the words after you.

Display a <u>meterstick</u> and compare it to a centimeter ruler. **The meterstick is used to measure larger things than a centimeter ruler. A <u>meter</u> is a little longer than a yardstick.** Write the word "meter" on the board and have children repeat the word after you. **Which should we use to measure the length of a pencil—a centimeter ruler or a meterstick?** *(Centimeter ruler)* **A window?** *(Meterstick)*

Make two columns on the board with "centimeter ruler" and "meterstick" as the heads. Have children brainstorm items that can be measured with each. List reasonable items in the appropriate column.

Problem-Solving Strategy: Act It Out

ACCESS CONTENT; EXTEND LANGUAGE

Objective Solve problems involving perimeter by acting them out.

Materials *(per child)* Centimeter ruler; Centimeter Grid (Teaching Tool 37)

Vocabulary Perimeter

ESL Strategies   *Use before* LEARN   10 MIN

Use Small-Group ➤
Interactions

Have children work in pairs. Distribute the centimeter grid paper and centimeter rulers to children. Draw a rectangle on the board. Then have children draw a rectangle on the grid paper. Remind children to draw four straight lines that are connected to make a closed figure. Walk around the room to monitor children's work. Be sure children draw a figure with opposite parallel sides of the same length. When the figures have been drawn, have partners exchange papers. Inform children that they are going to find the <u>perimeter</u> of the rectangle.

Have Students Report Back in Writing ➤ **Use your centimeter rulers to find the length of each side of the rectangle. Write down each length. Measure all four lengths. Then add the four lengths together.** Call on pairs to give their answers. Explain to children that they have found the perimeter of the rectangle. Write the following rule for finding perimeter on the board. "To find the perimeter of a figure, add the length of all the sides." Invite children to read the rule aloud with you. In their notebooks, have children write how they could find the perimeter of the classroom. Encourage children to refer to the rule on the board to help them as they write in their notebooks.

Understanding Capacity

ACCESS CONTENT

USE WITH LESSON 9-6

Objective Estimate, measure, and order objects by their capacities, using nonstandard units.

Materials Paper cup; macaroni; cooking pot; containers of different sizes

Vocabulary Capacity

ESL Strategies **Use before** LEARN ⏱ 5–10 MIN

Use Real Objects ➤ Explain to children that they are going to learn about <u>capacity</u>. Write the word "capacity" on the board and invite children to repeat the term after you. *Capacity* **is the amount a container can hold. Containers come in different sizes.** Show a paper cup to the class and fill it with macaroni. Display a cooking pot. **Who thinks the pot will hold more macaroni than the cup?** Have children raise their hands. **Who thinks the pot will hold less macaroni than the cup?** Have children raise their hands. Pour the macaroni from the cup into the pot. Hold up the pot. **Which container can hold more macaroni?** *(The pot)* Have small groups repeat the activity using containers of various sizes.

Cups, Pints, and Quarts

ACTIVATE PRIOR KNOWLEDGE/BUILD BACKGROUND; EXTEND LANGUAGE

Objective Compare the capacities of cups, pints, and quarts.

Materials Cup, pint, and quart containers; water

Vocabulary Cup (c), pint (pt), quart (qt)

ESL Strategies   *Use before* LEARN   ⏱ 10 MIN

Connect to Prior Knowledge of Math ➤ Ask children if they remember what equal means. *(Sample answer: the same)* **How many inches equal 1 ft?** *(12)* **How many feet equal 1 yd?** *(3)* Explain that you can also show capacity with equal measures. Take out 1 <u>quart</u>, 2 <u>pint</u>, and 4 <u>cup</u> containers. Hold up the containers one at a time, and tell children the capacity of each one. Fill the quart container with water. **This container holds 1 qt.** Pour the water into the 2 pt containers. **How many pints equal 1 qt?** *(2)* Write "1 quart = 2 pints" on the board. **These containers each hold 1 pt.** Pour the water into the 4 c containers. **How many cups equal 2 pt?** *(4)* Write "= 4 cups" to the right of "2 pints." **How many cups equal 1 qt?** *(4)* Write "1 quart = 4 cups" on the board. **How many cups equal 1 pt?** *(2)* Write "1 pint = 2 cups" on the board.

Have Students Report Back in Writing ➤ Write the following problem on the board. Read the problem to the class. **"Toni wants to make 5 quarts of fruit punch. She does not have any quart containers. How can she make the punch?"**

If Toni used pint containers, how many would she need? *(10)* **If she used cup containers, how many would she need?** *(20)* Have children write how Toni can use pint or cup containers to make the punch. Encourage children to refer to the equations on the board and the words in the problem to help them articulate their responses.

Liters

ACCESS CONTENT

Objective Estimate and measure capacity in liters.

Materials Liter container; containers smaller than a liter; bucket; water

Vocabulary Liter (L)

ESL Strategies   *Use before* LEARN   ⏱ 5 MIN

Give Frequent Feedback ➤ Show children a <u>liter</u> container. **This container holds one L.** Write the word "liter" on the board and invite children to repeat the word after you. Fill the container with water. Point to a smaller container. **Will this container hold more or less than 1 L?** Invite children to share their ideas. Pour the water from the liter container into the smaller container. **Did the container hold more or less than 1 L?**

(Less) **How do you know?** *(There is still water left in the liter container.)* Point to the smaller container. **This container holds less than 1 L.** Pour the water back into the liter container and then point to a bucket. **Will this container hold more or less than 1 L?** Invite children to share their ideas. Pour the water from the liter container into the bucket. **Did the container hold more or less than 1 L?** *(More)* **How do you know?** *(There is room for more water in the bucket.)* **This container holds more than 1 L.**

Understanding Volume

USE WITH LESSON 9-9

ACTIVATE PRIOR KNOWLEDGE/BUILD BACKGROUND; ACCESS CONTENT

Objective Count and compare the numbers of cubes needed to build or fill various rectangular prisms.

Materials *(per group)* Cubes

Vocabulary Volume, cubic units

ESL Strategies

Use before CHECK ✓

⏱ 10–15 MIN

Connect to Prior Knowledge of Math ➤ Review the concept of capacity. **<u>Volume</u> is the amount of space inside a container. Volume is measured in <u>cubic units</u>.** Write "cubic units" on the board. **What word does** *cubic* **sound like?** *(Cube)* **Is a cube a plane figure or a solid figure?** *(Solid figure)* Show a cube to children. **How many faces does a cube have?** *(6)* **What figure is each face of the cube?** *(Square)* **What do you notice about the height, width, and length of a cube?**

Use Manipulatives ➤ Divide the class into small groups and distribute cubes to each. Write "8 cubes, 10 cubes, 12 cubes, 16 cubes" on the board. Instruct children to make solid rectangular figures using the number of cubes written on the board. Have groups write the number of cubes for each layer and how many layers they have for each figure. Walk around the room to help groups construct their solid rectangular figures. Ask groups to explain how they made their solid rectangular figures.

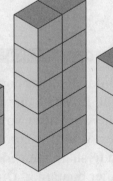
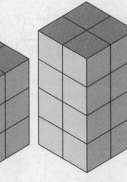

8 Cubic Units   10 Cubic Units   12 Cubic Units   16 Cubic Units

Understanding Weight

ACCESS CONTENT

Objective Estimate and measure the weights of different objects by comparing each of them to a nonstandard unit of weight.

Materials Balance scale; textbook; scissors; box of crayons

Vocabulary Weight

ESL Strategies   *Use before* **LEARN**   ⏱ 10 MIN

Use Real Objects ➤ **What do we mean when we talk about the <u>weight</u> of something?** *(How heavy something is)* Write the phrases "weigh more" and "weigh less" on the board. Ask children to repeat each phrase after you. Discuss the phrases with children to make sure they understand what each one means. Then place a math book on the balance scale. Hold up a pair of scissors. **Who thinks the scissors will weigh more than the book? Who thinks the scissors will weigh less than the book?** Place the scissors on the balance scale. **Do the scissors weigh more or less than the book?** *(Sample Answer: The scissors weigh less than the book.)* Remove the book and hold up a box of crayons. Repeat the activity, asking children to predict whether the box of crayons will weigh more or less than the scissors.

Pounds and Ounces

ACCESS CONTENT

Objective Compare and estimate the weights of objects in ounces and pounds.

Materials Balance scale; *(per group)* 1-pound can of fruit or vegetables

Vocabulary Pound (lb), ounce (oz)

ESL Strategies   *Use before* **CHECK** ✓   ⏱ 5–10 MIN

Use Real Objects ➤ Divide the class into groups of three children. Give each group a 1-<u>pound</u> can of fruit or vegetables to pass around. **How much do you think this can weighs?** Then tell children the can weighs 1 lb. Write "1 pound" on the board. **Was it hard or easy to pick up 1 lb?** *(Easy)* **Do you think your desk** weighs more or less than the can you just picked up? *(More)* **Your desk weighs more than 1 lb.**

Discuss that an <u>ounce</u> is part of a pound. Write "1 pound = 16 ounces" on the board. **Repeat after me: One pound equals 16 ounces.** Have children pick up their pencils. **Do you think your pencil weighs closer to a pound or an ounce?** *(Ounce)* Place the pencil on one side of the balance scale with the can on the other side. **How many pencils equal one pound?** Continue to put pencils on the balance scale until the scale balances. When the scale balances, say: **(Insert number) pencils equal 1 pound.**

Grams and Kilograms

USE WITH LESSON 9-12

ACTIVATE PRIOR KNOWLEDGE/BUILD BACKGROUND; ACCESS CONTENT

Objective Compare and estimate the masses of objects in grams and kilograms.

Materials 220 pieces of $8\frac{1}{2}$" × 11" paper or a little less than half a ream; a little less than $\frac{1}{4}$ of a piece of $8\frac{1}{2}$" × 11" paper; large book; baseball cap

Vocabulary Gram, kilogram

ESL Strategies   ***Use before*** **LEARN**   ⏱ 10 MIN

Connect to Prior Knowledge of Math ➤ Review the concepts of pounds and ounces with children. Then tell them them that they are going to be learning about other units called grams and <u>kilograms</u>. Write the words "gram" and "kilogram" on the board, and invite children to repeat the terms after you. Explain that the measure of 1 g is less than an ounce and the measure of 1 kg is more than a pound.

Give Frequent Feedback ➤ Display a piece of paper that is a little less than $\frac{1}{4}$ of a $8\frac{1}{2}$" × 11" sheet. **Do you think this piece of paper weighs closer to 1 g or 1 kg?** *(1 g)* **This piece of paper measures about 1 g.** Display 220 sheets of $8\frac{1}{2}$" × 11" paper. **This entire stack of paper weighs about 1,000 g or 1 kg. 1,000 g equal 1 kg.** Write "1,000 grams = 1 kilogram" on the board. Invite children to lift the stack of paper so they can feel the approximate weight of a kilogram. Let children lift the piece of paper to compare how 1 gram feels compared to 1 kilogram. Display a baseball cap. **Is the cap more or less than 1 kg?** *(Less)* **Do you think you are more or less than 1 kg?** *(More)* Continue asking questions about light and heavy objects.

Temperature: Fahrenheit and Celsius

USE WITH LESSON 9-13

ACTIVATE PRIOR KNOWLEDGE/BUILD BACKGROUND; EXTEND LANGUAGE

Objective Show, read, and write temperatures shown on Fahrenheit and Celsius thermometers.

Materials Thermometer (Teaching Tool 39)

Vocabulary Temperature, degrees, Fahrenheit (°F), Celsius (°C)

ESL Strategies

Use before LEARN

🕐 10–15 MIN

Connect to Prior Experiences ➤ Ask children if they have ever watched the weather on the news or discussed it with their families. Talk about the different <u>temperatures</u> it might have been outside when they played in the snow or went swimming. **To measure temperature, we use units called <u>degrees</u>. The United States uses degrees <u>Fahrenheit</u>, while most of the world uses degrees <u>Celsius</u>.** Write "degrees Fahrenheit (°F)" and "degrees Celsius (°C)" on the board. Have children say the terms with you. Point out that we often see the abbreviated versions on a thermometer.

Draw a thermometer on the board. **It needs to be 32°F or colder to snow.** On one side of the thermometer, label it "32°F". **It needs to be 0°C or colder to snow.** Label the other side of the thermometer "0°C." Point out that these readings are the same temperature. Have children write about the things they would do if the weather were 32°F or 0°C and snowy outside. Have them include in their reports both the outside temperature and a drawing of a thermometer showing that temperature. Make sure their thermometers are labeled in both degrees Fahrenheit and degrees Celsius. When children have finished, read some of the reports to the class.

Understanding Probability

USE WITH LESSON 9-14

EXTEND LANGUAGE

Objective Predict the outcomes of simple experiments.

Materials *(per pair)* Red and yellow two-color counters

Vocabulary More likely, less likely, equally likely

ESL Strategies

Use before CHECK ✓

🕐 15 MIN

Focus on Meaning ➤ Say the word "probably" and write it on the board. Invite children to read the word with you. Have a volunteer explain the meaning of the word. *(A good chance that something will happen.)* Then write the word "likely" on the board. **Do you think the words *probably* and *likely* mean the same thing or the opposite thing?** *(The same thing)* Then review the meanings of the words *more*, *less*, and *equal*. Discuss how those words can be used with *likely* to compare probabilities. **On Tuesday you will probably be at school. So are** you <u>more likely</u> or <u>less likely</u> to be at school? *(More likely)* **Is it more likely to snow in Florida than in Alaska, or less likely to snow in Florida than in Alaska?** *(Less likely)* Ask a volunteer to name something that is <u>equally likely</u>. *(Sample answer: getting heads or tails when tossing a coin)*

Have Students ➤ Report Back in Writing

Divide the class into pairs, and distribute red and yellow counters to each pair. Have each pair write three scenarios using the terms *more likely*, *less likely*, and *equally likely* to describe the probability of picking a red counter versus a yellow counter. Write the following sentence stem on the board for children to use as a model. "We are _____ to pick a _____ counter than a _____ counter." Also write the terms "more likely," "less likely," and "equally likely" on the board to remind pairs to use them in their writing. Have them include a drawing of the counters in their reports.

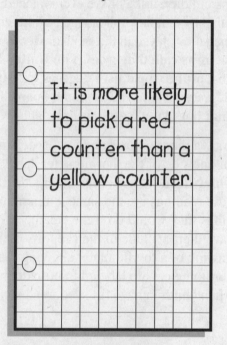

It is more likely to pick a red counter than a yellow counter.

Using Probability

ACTIVATE PRIOR KNOWLEDGE/BUILD BACKGROUND; ACCESS CONTENT

Objective Record and analyze data collected from performing an experiment.

Materials *(per group)* Penny; lined paper numbered 1–20 with columns labeled "heads", "tails," and "other"

Vocabulary Certain, probable, impossible

ESL Strategies — *Use before* ▮LEARN▮   🕐 10 MIN

Use Brainstorming ➤ Write the words "certain" "probable", and "impossible" on the board. Discuss the meaning of each word and invite children to predict events in everyday life that would fall under each category. Write them on the board under each word.

Use Small-Group Interactions ➤ Divide the class into groups and distribute a penny and a sheet of paper numbered 1–20 with columns labeled "heads", "tails", and "other". **We are going to conduct an experiment. What does *experiment* mean?** *(Encourage all responses.)* An experiment tests an idea, or prediction, in real life. **We are going to toss a penny 20 times and record how it lands: heads or tails.** Write the following sentence frames on the board.

It is certain that _____. *(Sample answer: the coin will land heads, tails, or on its edge.)*

It is probable that _____. *(Sample answer: it will land on tails ten times.)*

It is impossible that _____. *(Sample answer: the coin will land on the ceiling.)*

Have each group use the sentence frames to make their predictions. Visit each group and help them by asking questions such as, **How many times do you think the coin will land on heads? Land on tails? Roll into the playground?** Have group members take turns tossing the coin and recording the results until they have completed 20 trials. Have groups share their predictions and results.

	Heads	Tails	Other
1.	x		
2.	x		
3.		x	
4.	x		
5.		x	
6.	x		
7.	x		
8.		x	
9.	x		
10.		x	
11.	x		
12.	x		
13.	x		
14.		x	
15.		x	
16.		x	
17.		x	
18.	x		
19.		x	
20.		x	

Problem-Solving Skill: Multiple-Step Problems

ACCESS CONTENT

Objective Solve multiple-step problems involving addition and subtraction.

Materials *(per group)* Two-color counters

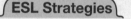
ESL Strategies

Expand Student ➤
Responses

Use before CHECK ✓

⏱ 10 MIN

Write the following problem on the board and read it aloud. "Pedro has 30 counters. 18 of the counters are red. The rest are yellow. How many more red counters does he have than yellow counters?"

What do we need to find? *(How many more red counters Pedro has than yellow counters)* **What do we know?** *(There are 30 counters and 18 of the counters are red. The other counters are all yellow.)* **What is the first thing we need to find?** *(The number of yellow counters)* **How can we do that?** *(Subtract the number of red counters from all the counters: 30 − 18 = 12)* **What do we need to do next to answer the question?** *(Subtract the number of yellow counters from the number of red counters: 18 − 12 = 6)* **How many more red counters does Pedro have than yellow counters?** *(6 more red counters)*

Divide the class into pairs. Have each child write a multiple-step problem to give to his or her partner to solve. Check that problems are solvable.

30 total counters − 18 red counters = 12 yellow counters
18 − 12 = 6 more red counters

Problem-Solving Applications:
How Do You Measure Up?

EXTEND LANGUAGE

Objective Review and apply key concepts, skills, and strategies learned in this and previous chapters.

ESL Strategies

Use before **CHECK ✓**

⏱ 10 MIN

Have Students ➤
Create Test Items

Divide the class into pairs. Have them read to each other the Writing in Math story they wrote in their journals about a time when it was important to measure the length or weight of something. Then ask them to write any questions about measurement that they found in their partners' story.

Ask several volunteers to come to the board to write a problem about measurement from the stories they heard or read. Ask children to identify how they would measure the items in the stories using what they have learned from this chapter. Have volunteers show the solutions to their problems on the board, using help from the class when needed.

Building 1,000

USE WITH LESSON **10-1**

ACTIVATE PRIOR KNOWLEDGE/BUILD BACKGROUND; ACCESS CONTENT

Objective Count by hundreds to 1,000.

Materials *(per pair)* Place-Value Blocks (Teaching Tool 40)

Vocabulary Hundreds, thousand

ESL Strategies   *Use before* ▌LEARN▐   ⏱ 10 MIN

Connect to Prior Knowledge of Math ➤

Tell children that they are going to make one <u>thousand</u>. **How many ones are there in 10?** *(10)* Write "10 = 10 ones" on the board. **How many tens are there in 100?** *(10)* Write "100 = 10 tens." Hold up a hundred place-value block and a thousand place-value block. **Which block is bigger, the hundred place-value block or the thousand place-value block?** *(Thousand)* Write "thousand" on the board and invite children to repeat the word after you. **If there are 10 ones in 10 and 10 tens in 100, how many hundreds do you think there are in 1,000?** *(10)* Write "1,000 = 10 hundreds" on the board. Then have the class skip count with you by 100s from 100 to 1,000. **One hundred, two hundred, . . . one thousand.**

Use Manipulatives ➤

Divide the class into pairs and distribute place-value blocks. Write 400 + 600 = 1,000 on the board. Then have the class say with you: **Four hundred plus six hundred equals one thousand.** Have pairs write other number sentences that show 1,000 as a sum and two addends that are both multiples of 100. Tell pairs to use the place-value blocks to help them write their number sentences. When children have finished, ask volunteers to name their answers.

Counting Hundreds, Tens, and Ones

USE WITH LESSON **10-2**

ACTIVATE PRIOR KNOWLEDGE/BUILD BACKGROUND; ACCESS CONTENT

Objective Count sets grouped in hundreds, tens, and ones.

Materials *(per pair)* Place-Value Blocks (Teaching Tool 40); Place-Value Mat B (Workmat 5)

Vocabulary Digit

ESL Strategies   *Use before* ▌LEARN▐   ⏱ 10 MIN

Connect to Prior Knowledge of Math ➤

Write 34 on the board. **How many tens are there in 34?** *(3)* **How many ones are there in 34?** *(34)* **What number does the <u>digit</u> 3 stand for?** *(30)* **Why?** *(The 3 is in the tens place.)* **What number does the *digit* 4 stand for?** *(4)* **Why?** *(The 4 is in the ones place.)*

Use Manipulatives ➤ Display 5 hundreds models. **How many hundreds are there?** *(5)* Encourage children to respond with complete sentences: "There are 5 hundreds." Combine the 5 hundreds models with 6 tens and 2 ones. Draw Workmat 5 on the board and have children tell which digit goes in which place.

Use Small-Group Interactions ➤ Divide children into pairs, and distribute the place-value blocks to each. Pairs should make three-digit numbers and write the digit that goes into each place. Have pairs use Workmat 5 to show each place in their 3-digit numbers. Have pairs ask each other, "Which number goes in the hundreds place?" "Which number goes in the tens place?" "Which number goes in the ones place?"

Writing Numbers to 1,000

USE WITH LESSON
10-3

ACCESS CONTENT

Objective Read and write three-digit numbers using expanded form, standard form, and number words.

Materials *(per group)* 3 index cards

Vocabulary Standard form, expanded form, number word

ESL Strategies | *Use before* CHECK ✓ | 10 MIN

Use Small-Group Interactions ➤ Divide the class into groups of three, and give each child three index cards. On each of the cards, have one group member write a three-digit number in <u>standard form</u>, have one member write a three-digit number in <u>expanded form</u>, and have the other member write 3 three-digit numbers using <u>number words</u>. You might have a child who is more proficient in English write the number words. Have one member of each group collect the cards, mix them up, and distribute one card to each member of the group. Each child should write the number on the card in a different form than is already there. Instruct children to write their responses on the same index card. When each member has finished, have the group discuss the answers. Then have a group member mix the cards again, and this time have children write the number form that is missing from the card.

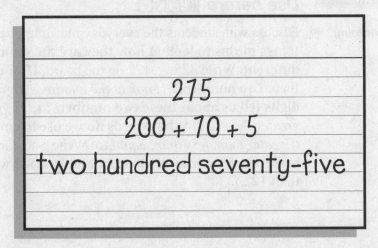

275
200 + 70 + 5
two hundred seventy-five

Changing Numbers by Hundreds and Tens

EXTEND LANGUAGE

Objective Add and subtract multiples of 10 or 100 to and from a three-digit number without regrouping.

Materials *(per pair)* Place-Value Mat B (Workmat 5)

ESL Strategies — *Use before* LEARN ⏱ 15 MIN

Have Students Report Back Orally ➤ Group the class into pairs. Write the following problems on the board:

325 + 40	782 − 500
325 + 400	782 − 50

Have children work together in pairs to find the sums and differences. Have pairs write the expanded forms of each number, using Workmat 5 to help them compute. When pairs have finished finding the sums and differences, have them explain in writing how they used the place value of the digits when adding and subtracting.

Have Students Create Test Items ➤ Invite pairs of children to write two more addition problems and two more subtraction problems like the ones above. When pairs have finished, collect the papers to give to other pairs. Then have the children work out the sums and differences. As pairs are working, walk around to monitor if they are correctly using place value in their adding and subtracting.

Comparing Numbers

EXTEND LANGUAGE

Objective Compare three-digit numbers using the symbols <, >, and =.

Materials *(per pair)* 6 index cards with 3-digit numbers written on them

Vocabulary Compare, greater than (>), less than (<), equal to (=)

ESL Strategies — *Use before* CHECK ✓ ⏱ 10 MIN

Focus on Meaning ➤ Discuss with students the everyday meaning of <u>compare</u>. **To compare two things means to look at how they are the same and how they are different.** Write 325 __ 122 on the board. **How do we compare the size of these two numbers?** *(Look at the hundreds digit.)* **What do the hundreds digits tell us about these two numbers?** *(3 is <u>greater than</u> 1, so 325 is greater than 122)* **What words do we use to compare the size of numbers?** *(Greater than, less than, equal to)* Write > to complete the inequality on the board. Have students read the inequality aloud with you, **"325 is greater than 122."**

Have children work in pairs. Give each pair of children 6 index cards with
3-digit numbers written on them and place the cards in a pile face down
between the partners. Have each partner draw a number at the same time,
then compare the pair of numbers by writing an inequality (or equality) in
symbols and in words. Each child should write the inequality with the
number he or she drew as the first term. Make sure children understand that
each round will result in two inequalities (unless the numbers are equal), for
example: "458 is greater than 241" and "241 is less than 458." Repeat until
all of the cards are drawn. Post this reminder on the board.

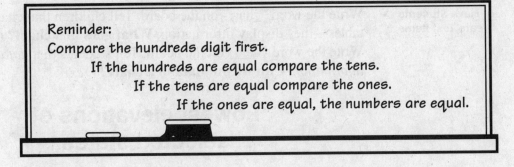

Reminder:
Compare the hundreds digit first.
　　If the hundreds are equal compare the tens.
　　　　If the tens are equal compare the ones.
　　　　　　If the ones are equal, the numbers are equal.

Visit each pair to help them compare numbers. If pairs finish early, they can
shuffle the index cards and play again.

Parts of 1,000

USE WITH LESSON
10-6

ACCESS CONTENT

Objective Use counting on to find missing parts of 1,000.

Materials *(per pair)* Play money

ESL Strategies **Use before** **LEARN** ⏱ 10 MIN

Use Manipulatives ➤ Have children make the connection between skip-counting numbers and
counting money. Have students work in pairs and play the roles of a bank
customer withdrawing funds and a bank teller. Give each customer one of the
following amounts: $550, $600, $650, $700, $750, $800, and $850. Give
each teller 4 hundred-dollar bills, and 10 ten-dollar bills.

Have customers use this sentence frame: "I have $ _____ . I need $1,000."
Bank tellers should hand the customers their bills one at a time, counting on
aloud by $100s then by $10s to make $1,000. Have students exchange roles
and redistribute the bills.

Problem-Solving Skill:
Use Data from a Chart

EXTEND LANGUAGE

Objective Use data from a chart to solve problems.

Materials Chart; data

ESL Strategies

Use before CHECK ✓

🕐 10–15 MIN

Have Students ➤ Create Test Items

Write the word "<u>chart</u>" on the board. Tell children that charts are like tables—they display information. **What goes in a chart?** *(Information)* Write the word "<u>data</u>" on the board. Tell students that *data* means information. **Can we put data in a chart?** *(Yes)*

Lowest elevations of selected states

State	Elevation (in feet)
Idaho	710
Iowa	480
Nebraska	840
Ohio	455
West Virginia	240

Divide the class into pairs. Try to pair English language learners with students who are more proficient in English. Explain that elevation is the height of any point above the level of the sea. You might want to demonstrate this concept by drawing a picture or a diagram on the board. Have each pair write 5 questions that can be asked and answered from the chart. For example: "How many feet are there between the two lowest elevations on the chart?" Go around to each pair and have them read a question from their list. Have pairs trade questions to answer.

Before, After, and Between

EXTEND LANGUAGE

Objective Identify numbers that are before, after, or between given numbers.

Materials *(per group)* Spinner

Vocabulary Before, after, between

ESL Strategies

Use before **LEARN**

⏱ 5 MIN

Focus on Meaning ➤ **What does *before* mean?** *(Sample answer: In front of)* **What number comes before 2?** *(1)* Write 732 on the board. Say the number with the class: **Seven hundred thirty-two. What number comes before 732?** *(731)* Write 731 to the left of 732 on the board. Say with the class: **Seven hundred thirty-one comes before seven hundred thirty-two. What does *after* mean?** *(Sample answer: Following)* **What number comes after 2?** *(3)* **What number comes after 732?** *(733)* Write 733 to the right of 732 on the board. Say with the class: **Seven hundred thirty-three comes after seven hundred thirty-two.** Underline 732 and say with the class: **Seven hundred thirty-two is <u>between</u> seven hundred thirty-one and seven hundred thirty-three.**

Divide the class into small groups, and give each group a spinner divided into 10 equal sections and labeled 0–9. Have each child spin the spinner three times to make a three-digit number. The result of the first spin indicates the hundreds place, the second spin indicates the tens place, and the third spin indicates the ones place. Have each child write the number that comes before and after that number. Write the following sentence stems on the board and have children fill in the blanks with their numbers.

My number is _____ .

_____ is before _____ .

_____ is after _____ .

_____ is between _____ and _____ .

Ordering Numbers

EXTEND LANGUAGE; ACCESS CONTENT

Objective Order three-digit numbers from greatest to least and from least to greatest.

Materials Index cards

Vocabulary Order, greatest, least

ESL Strategies

Use before CHECK ✓

🕐 10–15 MIN

Focus on Meaning ➤ Write the word _order_ on the board, and invite students to repeat the word after you. Have three volunteers come to the front of the room. **We can arrange the children in order from tallest to shortest. Who is the tallest?** Have that child stand on the left. **Who is the shortest?** Have that child stand on the right, and have the third child stand in the middle. **We ordered this group from tallest to shortest, or from the _greatest_ height to the _least_ height. In what other ways could the children have been ordered?** _(Sample answers: Shortest to tallest, alphabetical order, youngest to oldest)_

Use Small-Group Interactions ➤ Divide the class into groups of four or five. Distribute an index card to each child, and have him or her write a three-digit number on the index card. Then have the group order their index cards from the least number to the greatest number. Call upon a group to come to the front of the class and display their numbers. Have the children in the group order themselves from left to right and from the least number to the greatest number. Repeat with other groups alternating instructions from least to greatest and greatest to least.

Problem-Solving Strategy: Look for a Pattern

EXTEND LANGUAGE; ACCESS CONTENT

Objective Continue number patterns using three-digit numbers and skip count by different amounts.

Vocabulary Pattern, increase, decrease

ESL Strategies *Use before* **CHECK** ✓   ⏱ 10–15 MIN

Focus on Meaning ➤ Tell children that you are going to write a number <u>pattern</u> on the board. **What is a number pattern?** *(Sample answer: Numbers that continue by following a rule)* Write the numbers 103, 203, 303, 403, 503, 603 on the board. Read the numbers aloud with children. **What is the next number in the pattern?** *(703)* **How do you know?** *(The numbers go up by 100. 603 + 100 = 703)* Write the word "<u>increase</u>" on the board and invite children to repeat the word after you. **What does *increase* mean?** *(To go up)* **How did the numbers increase?** *(The numbers increased by 100.)* **The numbers in the pattern go up by 100, so they increase by 100.**

Ask children if they know a word that means the opposite of *increase*? *(Decrease)* **What does *decrease* mean?** *(To go down)* Write 450 on the board. **If the pattern is to decrease by 50, what are the next two numbers?** *(400 and 350)* Elicit from children that in this case decrease means to subtract by 50. Write 450 – 50 = 400; 400 – 50 = 350.

Use Small-Group ➤ Organize children into small groups. Write 360 on the board, and have **Interactions** each member of the group write a pattern involving 360. In turns, have one member read his or her numbers to the group. The other members discuss the rule of the pattern and find the next number. Continue the activity with other numbers that the group chooses. Walk around the room and ask, as appropriate: **Did the pattern increase? Did the pattern decrease? How did the pattern increase? How did the pattern decrease?**

Problem-Solving Applications: Rescue Vehicles

EXTEND LANGUAGE

Objective Review and apply key concepts, skills, and strategies learned in this and previous chapters.

ESL Strategies | *Use before* CHECK ✓ | 🕑 5–10 MIN

Have Students ➤ Create Test Items

Divide the class into pairs. Try to pair English language learners with students who are more proficient in English. Have partners read to each other the Writing in Math story they wrote in their journals about ordering numbers. Then ask them to write in their own words questions about writing, comparing, or ordering numbers that they found in their partners' stories in their journals.

Ask several volunteers to come to the board and write a problem about ordering numbers from the stories that they read. Ask children to identify the way they would write, compare, or order the numbers in the stories, based on what they have learned from this chapter.

Using Mental Math

USE WITH LESSON 11-1

EXTEND LANGUAGE; ACCESS CONTENT

Objective Add three-digit numbers mentally, without regrouping.

Materials *(per group)* Number cube

Vocabulary Three-digit number

ESL Strategies

Use before CHECK ✓   ⏱ 10 MIN

Have Students ➤ Report Back in Writing

Write 673 on the board. Have a volunteer say the expanded form aloud as you write it on the board. *(600 + 70 + 3)* Then write + 125 beneath 673 on the board. Ask another volunteer to say the expanded form of 125 and write the correct response on the board. *(100 + 20 + 5)* Ask children to explain in writing how they can use mental math to add the numbers. *(Add the hundreds, the tens, and the ones of the expanded numbers. Then add those sums together.)*

Use Small-Group ➤ Interactions

Divide the class into groups of four, and distribute 3 number cubes to each group. Have groups label their number cubes 0–5. Have one member toss the cubes to make a three-digit number. Tell the child to use the number that shows up on each cube as a digit in his or her number. Then have another member toss the cubes again to make a three-digit number to add to the first one. Tell children not to use two 5s in the same place value. Have children help each other to add and explain how they got their answer. When groups have finished, have a member from each group write their problem on the board.

$$
\begin{array}{r}
673 \\
+125 \\
\hline
798
\end{array}
$$

Hundreds
$$
\begin{array}{r}
600 \\
+100 \\
\hline
700
\end{array}
$$

Tens
$$
\begin{array}{r}
70 \\
+20 \\
\hline
90
\end{array}
$$

Ones
$$
\begin{array}{r}
3 \\
+5 \\
\hline
8
\end{array}
$$

Estimating Sums

USE WITH LESSON 11-2

EXTEND LANGUAGE; ACCESS CONTENT

Objective Decide whether the sum of 2 three-digit numbers is more or less than a given number.

Vocabulary Estimate

ESL Strategies **Use before** CHECK ✓   ⏱ 10 MIN

Focus on Meaning ➤ **You use the word <u>estimate</u> to mean about how much. Do you think an estimate is an exact answer?** *(No)* Give an example of an estimate and then an exact answer of a problem, such as 37 + 24, on the board. *(Estimate—60; exact answer—61)*

Use Small-Group ➤ Write 436 + 342 on the board. Have children work in pairs to estimate the
Interactions   sum to the nearest ten. Walk around the room and ask pairs to think of how they can tell whether 436 is closer to 430 or 440, and whether 342 is closer to 340 or 350. When pairs have finished, have a group explain their answer.

Write 586 + 219 on the board. Have pairs estimate the sum to the nearest hundred. Ask them if they think that the actual sum will be more than or less than 700. *(Sample answer: The estimated sum is 800, so the actual sum will be more than 700.)*

Adding with Models

USE WITH LESSON 11-3

ACCESS CONTENT

Objective Use place-value models to add 2 three-digit numbers with regrouping.

Materials *(per pair)* Place-Value Blocks (Teaching Tool 40)

Vocabulary Regroup

ESL Strategies **Use before** LEARN   ⏱ 10 MIN

Use Manipulatives ➤ Pair up children and distribute place-value blocks. Write 246 on the board and have one student in each pair model the number with the place-value blocks. **What blocks did you use to model this number?** *(2 hundreds, 4 tens, and 6 ones)* Then write + 376 next to 246, and have the other student in each pair model the second addend. **What blocks did you use to model this number?** *(3 hundreds, 7 tens, and 6 ones)* Using models, have children find the sum of both numbers. Ask volunteers to answer the following in complete sentences: **How many ones are there altogether?** *(There are 12 ones altogether.)* **Do you have to <u>regroup</u> ones to exchange for a ten?** *(Yes)* Tell children to regroup. **How many tens are there altogether?** *(There are 12 tens altogether.)* **Do you have to regroup tens**

to exchange for a hundred? *(Yes)* Tell children to regroup. **How many hundreds are in the sum?** *(There are 6 hundreds in the sum.)* **How many tens are in the sum?** *(2)* **What is the sum?** *(The sum is 622.)*

Use ➤
Peer Questioning

Give each pair a second addition problem to work on, and have each partner model one of the addends with the place-value blocks. Using the questions above ("How many ones/tens/hundreds do you have altogether? How did you regroup the ones/tens?" etc.), partners should discuss how they modeled the addend. Pairs then repeat the process for a third problem, with the other partner asking the questions.

Adding Three-Digit Numbers

USE WITH LESSON 11-4

EXTEND LANGUAGE; ACCESS CONTENT

Objective Use paper and pencil to add 2 three-digit numbers with one regrouping.

Materials *(per pair)* Place-Value Mat B (Workmat 5)

ESL Strategies ➤ **Use before** **LEARN**   ⏱ 10 MIN

Use ➤
Peer Questioning

What does it mean to *group* things? *(To organize or arrange)* **A prefix is a set of letters that is added to the beginning of a word. The prefix *re-* can be added to the beginning of the word *group*. If the prefix *re-* means again, what do you think the word *regroup* means?** *(To group again)*

Discuss the word *regroup* in relation to adding. Write 263 + 458 on the board. **What is 3 ones plus 8 ones?** *(11 ones)* **We have too many ones, so we have to regroup. How can we regroup 11 ones?** *(1 ten and 1 one)* On the board, write 1 in the ones place and add 1 to the tens place. **Now how many tens do we have?** *(12 tens)* **Do we need to regroup?** *(Yes)* **How can we regroup 12 tens?** *(1 hundred and 2 tens)* On the board, write 2 in the tens place and add 1 to the hundreds place. **Do we need to regroup in the hundreds place?** *(No)* **Why not?** *(There are only 7 hundreds.)* **What is the final sum?** *(721)*

Use Small-Group ➤
Interactions

Distribute Workmat 5 to pairs of children. Write 338 + 519 on the board. Have pairs determine which place, if any, needs regrouping. Have pairs explain in writing how they regrouped. When children have finished, ask a volunteer to show how he or she found the sum.

Practice with
Three-Digit Addition

Objective Add 2 three-digit numbers in vertical form when they are given in horizontal form.

Materials *(per pair)* Place-Value Mat B (Workmat 5)

ESL Strategies *Use before* **LEARN**   10 MIN

Expand Student ➤ Write 227 + 438 on the board. Write the problem again in vertical form.
Responses **Why did I write the problem this way?** *(It lets you find the sum of each place value more easily.)* **Can you regroup any ones?** *(Yes, 7 ones + 8 ones = 15 ones. I can regroup 15 ones as 1 ten and 5 ones.)* **Can you regroup any tens?** *(No, 2 tens + 3 tens + 1 ten = 6 tens. 6 tens is less than 10 tens.)* **Can you regroup any hundreds?** *(No, 2 hundreds + 4 hundreds = 6 hundreds. 6 hundreds is less than 10 hundreds.)* **What is the sum?** *(5 + 60 + 600 = 665)*

Use Small-Group ➤ Have children work in groups, and give each group Workmat 5. Have each
Interactions group member write one problem involving addition of 2 three-digit numbers. Children take turns asking the questions from the table as the other members solve the problem together. Before children begin, read each question aloud with them. Review any words or concepts that children may not understand.

Problem-Solving Strategy:
Make a Graph

Objective Solve word problems by displaying information in a graph.

ESL Strategies *Use before* **CHECK** 10 MIN

Use ➤ Draw the graph as illustrated below on the board, but leave the bars out.
Demonstration

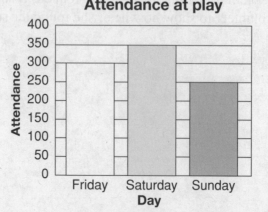

Attendance at play

Identify the different parts of the graph such as the title, the labels on each axis, and the scale. **300 people went to the play on Friday. How can we show on the graph how many people went?** Have a volunteer come to the board and draw a bar to 300, extending from the label "Friday." Continue with the attendance of 350 on Saturday and 250 on Sunday.

Have Students ➤ Divide the class into small groups. **400 people went to the show on**
Report Back **Monday. How does that change the graph?** Have each group write the
in Writing process for adding this information and have them make the new graph.

Ways to Find
Missing Parts

USE WITH LESSON
11-7

ACTIVATE PRIOR KNOWLEDGE/BUILD BACKGROUND

Objective Given a quantity and one of its parts, find the missing part by counting on or counting back.

ESL Strategies | *Use before* **LEARN** | ⏱ 10–15 MIN

Connect to Prior ➤ Draw a picture of an analog clock on the board and show the time 7:40. Ask
Knowledge of a volunteer to explain how to find the time shown by the minute hand.
Math *(Sample answer: Count back by fives from 60.)* As you point to the clock, have children count back from 60 to 40. **Is there another way we can find the same number?** *(Count on by fives from 0.)* As you point to the clock, have children count on by fives from 0 until 40.

Write 480 + _____ = 700 on the board. **In what two ways can you count to find the missing number?** *(Count on from 480 by hundreds and tens; count back from 700 by hundreds and tens.)* Have children work with a partner to count on from 480, or count back from 700 to find the missing number. When pairs have finished, have a pair explain how they found the missing number. Then have another pair describe how they used the other method.

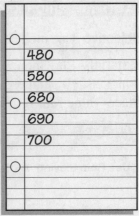

480
580
680
690
700

100, 200, 210, 220

Estimating Differences

USE WITH LESSON 11-8

Objective Use estimation to select two numbers that have a given difference.

ESL Strategies | ***Use before*** LEARN | 🕐 5 MIN

Connect to Prior
Knowledge of
Math
➤ Write $78 - 43$ on the board. Tell children that they are going to estimate the difference. **What do you do when you estimate?** *(You find about how much.)* Have children estimate to the nearest ten. **What subtraction problem can you write to estimate to the nearest ten?** *(80 − 40 = 40)* Write $80 - 40 = 40$ underneath $78 - 43$.

Have Students
Report Back
in Writing
➤ Write $678 - 262$ on the board. **We want to know about how much the difference is. Instead of finding each number to the nearest ten, find the number to the nearest hundred.** In their journals, have children write each of the numbers to the nearest hundred. Invite children to write a subtraction problem to estimate the difference. **About how much is the difference?** *(400)* Then have children write subtraction problems in which the estimated difference to the nearest hundred is 100, 200, 300, 400, and 500. Have volunteers read their subtraction problems to the class.

Subtracting with Models

USE WITH LESSON 11-9

Objective Use models to subtract three-digit numbers with regrouping.

Materials Play money: 1 five-dollar bill, 5 dollar bills, 2 quarters, 2 dimes, 4 nickels, 10 pennies; *(per group)* Place-Value Blocks (Teaching Tool 40); Place-Value Mat B (Workmat 5); Spinner (Teaching Tool 8)

ESL Strategies | ***Use before*** CHECK ✓ | 🕐 10–15 MIN

Use Role Playing
➤ Write the following items with prices on the board: "Kickball $1.70, Book $3.50, Pen $1.20."

Have two volunteers come to the front of the room. One will be a customer who will purchase one of the items with a $5 bill. The other will be a cashier. Have the customer say, "I would like to buy the (item) for (price)." Then have the customer hand the cashier the $5 bill. **How can we figure out how much money the customer gets back?** *(Subtract the price of the item purchased from $5.00.)* **We can think of 5 dollars as 500 pennies.** On the board write "$5.00 = 500 cents." **We can also turn the price of (item) into cents.** On the board, write the price of the item chosen in dollars and then in cents. Have children write the subtraction problem for the exchange between the customer and the cashier. *(For example, if the customer buys the pen, the subtraction problem would be 500 − 120.)* Have the cashier give the correct amount of change to the customer. *($3.80)*

Divide the class into small groups. Distribute the place-value blocks, Workmat 5, and a spinner to groups. Have the groups label the spinner with 8 different three-digit numbers. In turns, have the group members spin the spinner twice to get 2 three-digit numbers. The group members use the place-value blocks and Workmat 5 to model subtracting the lesser number from the greater number. Walk around the room to help groups with their regrouping or any other problems they may encounter.

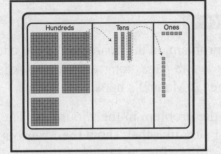
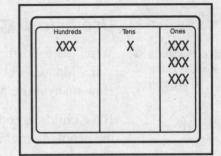

Subtracting Three-Digit Numbers

EXTEND LANGUAGE

USE WITH LESSON
11-10

Objective Use the standard algorithm to subtract three-digit numbers with regrouping.

Materials Place-Value Mat B (Workmat 5)

ESL Strategies *Use before* **CHECK** ✓   ⏱ 10 MIN

Have Students ➤
Report Back
Orally

Write the following problems on the board:

$$\begin{array}{r} 638 \\ -452 \\ \hline \end{array} \qquad \begin{array}{r} 915 \\ -308 \\ \hline \end{array} \qquad \begin{array}{r} 378 \\ -289 \\ \hline \end{array}$$

Have children work in pairs, and distribute Workmat 5. **We subtract three-digit numbers in the same way as we subtract two-digit numbers.** Have pairs copy the first problem, write which place needs regrouping, and explain why. *(The tens place needs regrouping. Three is smaller than 5, so there are not enough tens to subtract.)* Have a volunteer explain how to regroup 638. *(I can regroup 6 hundreds, 3 tens, 8 ones as 5 hundreds, 13 tens, 8 ones.)* Use slashes to show the regrouping on the board. **What is 638 minus 452?** *(1 hundred, 8 tens, 6 ones, or 186)* Have pairs work on the next two problems. When pairs have finished, have volunteer pairs explain their answers.

Practice with Three-Digit Subtraction

EXTEND LANGUAGE; ACCESS CONTENT

Objective Subtract three-digit numbers written in horizontal form.

Materials *(per group)* Posterboard

ESL Strategies

Use before CHECK ✓

⏱ 5–10 MIN

Have Students ➤
Report Back
in Writing

Write the following problem on the board and invite children to read it with you: "Manuel's book is 548 pages long. Anjali's book is 385 pages long. How many more pages is Manuel's book?"

Have children copy the problem in their journals. Then have them solve the problem, making sure that they show their regrouping. Walk around the room and ask the following questions as needed: **What numbers do you subtract?** *(548 – 385)* **How can you regroup 548 to subtract 385?** *(I can regroup 5 hundreds, 4 tens, 8 ones as 4 hundreds, 14 tens, 8 ones.)* When children have finished, have a volunteer give the answer using a complete sentence. *(Manuel's book has 163 more pages than Anjali's book.)*

Have children work in small groups to make a poster to explain how to use regrouping to subtract. The poster should include a word problem with subtraction of 2 three-digit numbers involving regrouping. There should also be a drawing that demonstrates the regrouping in the subtraction problem. Model an example like the one shown to help children get started.

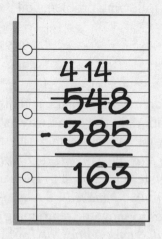

Problem-Solving Skill:
Exact Answer or Estimate?

USE WITH LESSON
11-12

ACCESS CONTENT; EXTEND LANGUAGE

Objective Distinguish between story problems that need exact answers and problems that need only estimated answers.

ESL Strategies *Use before* **LEARN**   ⏱ 5–10 MIN

Use Small-Group Interactions
> Write the following problem on the board: "The first grade sold 284 raffle tickets. The second grade sold 585 raffle tickets. Did the two grades sell more than 900 raffle tickets in all?"

Have children work in pairs to discuss the answer to the question. As children discuss the problem, suggest questions for them to ask: **Do we need an estimate or an exact answer? If we need an estimate, what numbers should we add?** Have pairs work together to write their answer. When pairs have finished writing, ask a pair to volunteer to explain how they found their answer.

Have Students Create Test Items
> Have each pair write two word problems, one with an estimated solution and one with an exact answer. When pairs have finished, collect the papers and distribute them to other pairs to solve. In their answers, pairs should explain why their answer is an exact answer or an estimate.

Problem-Solving Applications: Amazing Animals

EXTEND LANGUAGE

Objective Review and apply key concepts, skills, and strategies learned in this and previous chapters.

ESL Strategies   *Use before* **CHECK** ✓   ⏱ 5–10 MIN

Have Students Create Test Items ➤ Divide the class into pairs. Have children from each pair read to each other the Writing in Math story they wrote in their journals about flying tree snakes. Then have them write questions about adding three-digit numbers that they found in their partners' stories. They may also write subtraction problems that can be made from reading the story.

Ask several volunteers to come to the board and write a problem about adding or subtracting three-digit numbers from the stories they read. Ask children to identify from those problems the way they would add or subtract in the stories, based on what they have learned from this chapter.

Skip Counting Equal Groups

USE WITH LESSON **12-1**

EXTEND LANGUAGE; ACCESS CONTENT

Objective Make equal groups of objects and then find the total number of objects in those groups.

Vocabulary Equal groups

ESL Strategies **Use before** CHECK ✓ ⏱ 10 MIN

Focus on Meaning ➤ Write the word "equal" on the board and invite a volunteer to read the word for the class. **What does equal mean?** *(The same)* **What does <u>equal groups</u> mean?** *(Groups that have the same number)* Have children draw 4 equal groups of 3 circles and write the total number of circles that they have drawn. *(12)*

Use Small-Group ➤ Have children form groups of six. Instruct the groups that they will be skip
Interactions counting by various numbers, starting with 2. Have one member start the counting by saying "I have 2. The next number is 4." Going clockwise, have the next child say "I have 4. The next number is 6." Have the group continue until they reach 12. The last child should say "I have 12." Write 2, 4, 6, 8, 10, 12 on the board. Have the next group skip count by threes in the same fashion. When the group has finished skip counting by threes, write 3, 6, 9, 12, 15, 18 on the board. Continue skip counting by fours, fives, and sixes.

Repeated Addition
and Multiplication

ACCESS CONTENT

Objective Write equivalent repeated-addition and multiplication number sentences.

Materials *(per group)* 12 two-color counters

Vocabulary Multiplication sentence, multiply, times

ESL Strategies **Use before** CHECK ✓   ⏱ 10 MIN

Use Manipulatives ➤ Have children work in groups, and distribute 12 counters to each group. Have each group model 2 sets of 3 counters. **How many groups of 3 counters do you have?** *(2)* Write 3 and, below it, $3 \times 2 = 6$ on the board. **This multiplication sentence tells us to multiply 3 by 2 groups.** Have children say, "Three **times** two equals six". Then ask each group to model another set of 3 counters. **What addition sentence can I write to show the number of counters now?** *(3 + 3 + 3 = 9)* Write $3 + 3 + 3 = 9$ on the board. **What multiplication sentence can I write to show the number of counters?** *(3 × 3 = 9)* Write $3 \times 3 = 9$ below $3 + 3 + 3 = 9$, and have children say, "Three times three equals nine." Have children write the equations. Then ask each group to model a fourth set of 3 counters. **What addition sentence can I write to show the number of counters altogether?** *(3 + 3 + 3 + 3 = 12)* Write $3 + 3 + 3 + 3 = 12$ on the board. **What multiplication sentence can I write to show the number of counters?** *(3 × 4 = 12)* Write $3 \times 4 = 12$ below $3 + 3 + 3 + 3 = 12$, and have children say, "Three times four equals twelve." Have children write the equations.

Building Arrays

ACCESS CONTENT

Objective Build an array to model a multiplication situation.

Materials *(per child)* 20 two-color counters

Vocabulary Array

ESL Strategies **Use before** CHECK ✓   ⏱ 10–15 MIN

Use Manipulatives ➤ Have children work in pairs and distribute 20 counters to each child. Explain to children that they are going to make arrays with the counters based on the number that you call out. For example, call out the number 6, which means that they will use 6 counters to make an array. Pairs can make an array of 1 row with 6 counters in the row, 2 rows with 3 in each row, 3 rows with 2 in each row, or 6 rows of 1 counter each. Have pairs report aloud, using sentences such as "2 counters in each row times 3 rows equals 6 counters." Then have each child draw their array and write a multiplication sentence that describes it. Model an example if necessary. Repeat the activity using any of the following numbers. 4, 8, 9, 10, 12, 14, 15, 16, 18, 20.

Multiplying in Any Order

USE WITH LESSON 12-4

ACTIVATE PRIOR KNOWLEDGE/BUILD BACKGROUND; ACCESS CONTENT

Objective Multiply numbers in any order to get the same product.

Materials *(per child)* 15 two-color counters

ESL Strategies

Use before **LEARN** ⏱ 10 MIN

Connect to Prior Knowledge of Math ➤ Distribute 15 counters to each child. Write 5 + 3 = _____ on the board. Have children model the addition with their counters. **What is 5 plus 3?** *(8)* Ask children to model 3 + 5 with their counters. **What is 3 plus 5?** *(8)* **Does 5 + 3 equal 3 + 5?** *(Yes)* **Why?** *(Both expressions equal 8; changing the order of the numbers does not change the sum.)* Have the class say, "The order of the numbers does not change the sum." Remind children that multiplication is the same as adding over and over again. Divide the class into pairs. Have one partner make 5 equal groups of 3 counters and the other partner make 3 equal groups of 5 counters. Have partners write multiplication sentences to show each array. Invite volunteers to share their ideas about why the products were the same.

Use Manipulatives ➤ Have pairs use their counters to model other multiplication sentences where the order does not change the product. Tell pairs to write their multiplication sentences and draw arrays to represent them. When children have finished, ask volunteers to share their examples.

Vertical Form

USE WITH LESSON 12-5

ACTIVATE PRIOR KNOWLEDGE/BUILD BACKGROUND; EXTEND LANGUAGE

Objective Multiply numbers written in vertical format.

Vocabulary Vertical

ESL Strategies

Use before **LEARN** ⏱ 10–15 MIN

Connect to Prior Knowledge of Math ➤ Write 6 + 3 on the board in both <u>vertical</u> and horizontal forms. Ask two volunteers to come to the board to solve the problem. **Did the way I write the problem change the answer?** *(No)* **What is the sum of 6 + 3?** *(9)* Indicate which problem was written in vertical form and which was written in horizontal form. Use hand movements as you define vertical as up and down, and horizontal as across or as left to right. Draw 6 groups of 2 circles on the board. Have two more volunteers come to the board to write the multiplication sentence that describes the drawing. Have the child on the left write the problem vertically and the child on the right write the problem horizontally. **What is the product of 6 × 2?** *(12)* **Did the way they wrote the problems change the answer?** *(No)* **Was the problem on the left written in vertical form or in horizontal form?** *(Vertical)* **Was the problem on the right written in vertical form or in horizontal form?** *(Horizontal)*

Divide the class into pairs. Have each child write 5 multiplication problems in horizontal form. Instruct children to use only the numbers 2, 3, 4, 5, and 6 in their problems. Have children exchange papers with their partner when they have finished. Instruct each child to find the product of his or her partner's multiplication problems. Then have them write the problems vertically and find the products.

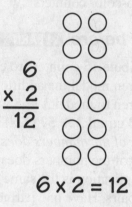

$$6$$
$$\times\ 2$$
$$\overline{12}$$

$$6 \times 2 = 12$$

Problem-Solving Strategy: Draw a Picture

ACCESS CONTENT; EXTEND LANGUAGE

USE WITH LESSON
12-6

Objective Solve a problem by drawing a picture.

Materials *(per child)* Crayons; paper

ESL Strategies   ***Use before* CHECK ✓**   ⏱ 10 MIN

Use Pictures ➤   Distribute paper and crayons to each child. Write the following problem on the board. Invite children to read the problem with you. "There are 3 trees. Each tree has 4 birds' nests in it. How many birds' nests are there in all?"

Tell children that they can draw a picture to help them solve the problem. Walk around the room as children draw their pictures and be sure each child draws 3 trees with 4 nests in each tree. Then have them write the corresponding multiplication sentence. When children have finished, ask a volunteer to write the multiplication sentence on the board. *(3 × 4 = 12 or 4 × 3 = 12)*

Have Students ➤
Report Back
in Writing

In pairs, have each child write a multiplication word problem using the numbers 2, 3, 4, 5, and 6. Then have partners exchange problems and solve them. Tell children that their answers should include a drawing and a multiplication sentence. Ask pairs to talk about how drawing a picture helped them to solve the problem.

Making Equal Groups

ACCESS CONTENT

Objective Divide a set of objects into a given number of equal groups.

Materials *(per group)* 16 index cards

Vocabulary Equal share

ESL Strategies **Use before** LEARN

⏱ 10–15 MIN

Use Real Objects ➤ Assign children to groups of four and have them sit in circles. If the class is not divisible by four, ask some children to join you and act as your helpers. Give each group a set of 16 index cards. Appoint a child from each group to distribute index cards to the other members of his or her group. Tell these children to be sure every member of their group gets the same number of cards. **Count your cards. How many cards did each person get?** *(4)* Explain that you are going to play again and that each group should pick a person to pass out the cards. Collect the index cards from the groups. Give each child who is distributing cards 12 index cards instead of 16. Have them give the members of their group the same number of cards. **Count your cards. How many cards did each person get?** *(3)* **Each time the cards were passed out, the members of each group received an** equal share **of the cards. What does this mean?** *(Everyone in a group got the same number of cards.)*

Writing Division Sentences

ACCESS CONTENT

Objective Write a division sentence to represent a sharing situation.

Materials 15 two-color counters

Vocabulary Divide, divided by, division sentence

⌐ESL Strategies⌐ *Use before* **LEARN**   ⏱ 5 MIN

Use Manipulatives ➤ Give each child 15 counters. **Use the counters to make 3 equal groups with the counters.** Show children how to make the equal groups. **How many counters are in each group?** *(5)* Explain that they have just <u>divided</u> 15 by 3. Write 15 ÷ 3 = 5 on the board. **This is a <u>division sentence</u>.** Have children use the counters again to make 5 equal groups. Ask them to write a division sentence to show what they did. *(15 ÷ 5 = 3)*

Use Small-Group ➤ Write 16 ÷ 4 = 4 on the board. Have children work in small groups to make
Interactions   up a story problem for the division sentence. Encourage children to draw pictures to represent their stories. Then have each group present its story problem to the class.

Problem-Solving Skill: Choose an Operation

ACTIVATE PRIOR KNOWLEDGE/BUILD BACKGROUND; ACCESS CONTENT

Objective Choose a number sentence to represent a problem situation.

⌐ESL Strategies⌐ *Use before* **CHECK** ✓   ⏱ 10–15 MIN

Use ➤ Review with children that they now have used the four operations: addition,
Brainstorming   subtraction, multiplication, and division. Ask the class to think about words in math problems that tell you which operation to use. Divide the class into groups to have them list the different words or phrases that indicate which operation to use. Draw a chart like the one below to help groups get started. When groups have finished, ask volunteers to share a word or phrase from their list. Add these to the chart on the board. Continue until there is at least one word in each column.

Use Small-Group ➤ Write the numbers 2, 4, 6, and 8 on the board. Using these numbers, have
Interactions   children work in groups of 4 to write an addition sentence, a subtraction sentence, a multiplication sentence, and a division sentence. Have them include a drawing for each number sentence.

Use Total ➤ When groups have finished, have them present their number sentences to the
Physical Response   class. As children read their sentences, tell the other groups to raise their left hand if the problem requires addition, their right hand if the problem requires subtraction. If it is a multiplication problem, have them raise both hands. If it is a division problem, have them stand up.

Words that tell which operation to use

	Addition	Subtraction	Multiplication	Division
in all				
altogether				
find the sum				
how many more				
find the difference				
how many are there				
find the product				
how many are in each group				
if they share equally				

Problem Solving Applications: Up, Up, and Away!

EXTEND LANGUAGE

Objective Review and apply key concepts, skills, and strategies learned in this and previous chapters.

ESL Strategies

Use before CHECK ✓

⏱ 10–15 MIN

Have Students ➤ **Create Test Items**

Divide the class into pairs. If possible, pair English language learners with a child who is fluent in English. Have them read to each other the Writing in Math story they wrote in their journal about airplanes. Then have them write questions about multiplying numbers that they found in their partner's story in their journal.

Ask several volunteers to come to the board to write a problem about multiplying numbers from the stories they read. Ask children to identify from those problems the way they would multiply in the stories, based on what they have learned from this chapter.

Repeat the procedure for addition, subtraction, and division.